Bible Fun Stuff

FOR AGES 7–9

Fun & Freaky Science

David C Cook
transforming lives together

FUN & FREAKY SCIENCE
Published by David C. Cook
4050 Lee Vance View
Colorado Springs, CO 80918 U.S.A.

David C. Cook Distribution Canada
55 Woodslee Avenue, Paris, Ontario, Canada N3L 3E5

David C. Cook U.K., Kingsway Communications
Eastbourne, East Sussex BN23 6NT, England

Written by Nancy Sutton
Cover Design by BMB Design/Scott Johnson
Interior Design by TrueBlue Design/Sandy Flewelling
Illustrations by Robbie Short, Michael Harvey, Sandy Flewelling

ISBN 978-1-4347-6723-3

First Printing 2009
Printed in the United States

1 2 3 4 5 6 7 8 9 10

David C. Cook
transforming lives together

TABLE OF CONTENTS

Introduction

Fun, science, and the Bible? ABSOLUTELY! Bring some common items such as a soft drink, magnets, candy, vinegar, or baking soda and put them to work with the activities in this resource and you've got a formula for fun and freaky Bible lessons that will be remembered long after the experiment is completed.

Turn your classroom into a science lab with these 26 dynamic science explorations. Your 7- to 9-year-old students will delve, dig, and detect astonishing things about the world God created. Each 10-minute lesson is a hands-on experience that will allow children to experiment with a variety of substances, materials, everyday objects, and common science tools.

Children this age have a wonderful sense of curiosity that will get a workout with these activities. It's hands-on learning where they explore and uncover the answers to their *what, why,* and *how* questions. And for you, we've included a "Why does it work?" section to put you ahead of the students and keep you in the know.

Put on your safety goggles and discover some laws of physics, chemistry, and geometry, while embedding truths from God's Word in young hearts and minds.

How to Use This Book

The 26 activities in this book can be done in any order and easily fit into any curriculum. Simply use the Scripture and Topic Index on page 110 to match a project with the lesson you're teaching. These activities also can be used as alternate Step Three activities in several curriculum lines: David C. Cook Bible-in-Life, Echoes, LifeLINKS to God, College Press, Reformation Press, Wesley, Anglican, and The Cross. If you have one of these lines, look through the Correlation Chart on page 111 and find the activity geared to your lesson. You'll use this new activity instead of one of the other Step Three activities listed in your teacher's guide. This book, when combined with *Rock the Room Games*, will give you a full year's worth of Step Three replacement activities for the elementary age group.

Please keep in mind:

- Children need basic guidelines given in a positive way. For example: listen first, then follow directions; touch, smell, poke, and feel only when asked; explore freely but safely; everyone helps clean-up; and so on.
- As children explore, remind them to share materials and keep the experiments in the area where they belong.
- Some experiments are messy. It's wise to keep basic supplies handy such as paper towels, newspapers or a shower curtain (for protecting the table or work area), and trash bags.
- Look ahead in each activity to the "End with a Bang" questions and consider using them as your students progress through the experiment.
- Some experiments work better in small groups, especially when an adult volunteer assists each group of kids.
- Children will be eager to show parents the experiment. Instead of putting everything away at the end of the time, keep a sample available for children to show off.
- Experimental results may differ if you alter or substitute ingredients and methods, allowing kids to figure out what went wrong and how to correct it. That's a valuable skill for life!

VOLCANO CREATIONS

An explosive example of creation!

Bible Basis: Genesis 1:1–31; Psalm 111:2, 7

MEMORY VERSE:
Do you not know? Have you not heard? The LORD is the everlasting God, the Creator of the ends of the earth.
Isaiah 40:28a

BIBLE BACKGROUND

Throughout the first chapter of Genesis, the time period for each element of creation is listed as "one day" (Gen. 1:5, 8, 13, 19, 23, 31). Debate continues among Christians as to the exact length of a day of creation. Some argue for a young earth, taking a day as a literal 24-hour period. The Hebrew word used for day is *yom*. This word is used throughout Scripture to refer to a one-night/day cycle of 24 hours. Jonah 1:17 reminds us that Jonah endured three days in the fish—obviously 24 hours and not thousands or millions of years.

Others focus on scientific and geological findings pointing to an old earth idea allowing millions of years for the Creation. Second Peter 3:8 states, "With the Lord a day is like a thousand years, and a thousand years are like a day." Whatever time frame is taken, the Creation is still an astonishing marvel that has no equal.

The Bible leaves no question about the Creator. Isaiah 40:28 reminds us, "Do you not know? Have you not heard? The LORD is the everlasting God, the Creator of the ends of the earth." Praise the God of creation and help the children develop a habit of praising their Creator.

Teacher Tips:

Make your volcanoes inside, but take them outside for the eruptions. Using a narrow-opening water bottle will cause the eruption to go up a few inches above the opening. With wider jars and cans, the eruption will foam over the edge, but you can add more soda to keep the eruption going longer.

Some children may feel anxious or fearful when you use words like "eruption" or "explosion." Remind them that although you say the experiment explodes, it's very safe and no one will be hurt.

If your class time is short, complete Investigation steps 1 and 2 ahead of time.

Variations to the Experiment:

Did you know there are three types of volcanoes? They are shield (low and shaped like a Roman shield on the ground, such as the Hawaiian volcanic chain), cinder cone (bowl-shaped crater, rarely over 1,000 ft. high, such as Sunset Crater in Arizona), and composite (tall, mountain-like, such as Mt. St. Helens and Mt. Fuji). You may want to have three different-sized jars or bottles to represent the three types of volcanoes. In addition, you might cut brown construction paper to wrap around each jar or bottle to create the look of the volcano.

Materials List:

- 1 c. baking soda
- Vinegar (1 c. for jar or can; 2–4 c. for bottles)
- Empty peanut butter jars, cans, or water bottles
- Foam plate or pie tin (1 per volcano)
- Optional: funnel (helpful if using bottles)
- Optional: red-flavored powdered drink mix (to create a lava-colored mixture)
- Optional: salt dough recipe (to cover 2–3 jars)
    - 6 c. flour
    - 2 c. salt
    - 4 Tbs. cooking oil
    - 2 c. water
    - Large mixing bowl

INVESTIGATION

1. Have the children work in groups to mix together the salt dough with their hands. This takes three or four minutes if you have the ingredients premeasured. If time is tight, you may choose to make this ahead of time and bring the dough to class, or use play dough.
2. Place each jar, can, or bottle on a firm foam plate or pie tin. Let the children form the dough around the sides of the can to create a volcano. Children may want to wash their hands after forming the volcanoes with the salty dough.
3. Take the volcanoes outside and set them a few feet apart from each other.
4. Pour the colored drink mix into each container.
5. If using jars or cans, fill them about half-full with the vinegar. If using bottles, fill them half or three-fourths full. Note: The closer the vinegar is filled to the top of the bottle, the more spray you'll have. But you'll have a harder time getting the baking soda into the bottle before it starts to react.
6. When you're ready, add the baking soda. You can add as much as one-fourth cup at a time. If you're using a bottle, use a funnel or paper rolled into a funnel (this allows the baking soda to quickly drain into the bottle). After the initial eruption is over, you can add more baking soda to reactivate it.

WHY DOES IT WORK?

Vinegar is a weak acid, called acetic acid. Baking soda, also called sodium bicarbonate, is a base—the chemical opposite of acids. When the vinegar and baking soda mix, a reaction takes place that produces a gas known as carbon dioxide. The carbon dioxide causes the fizzing and bubbling you see as the eruption begins.

END WITH A BANG

- What did you think would happen in this experiment?
- What caused the "lava" to come out of the volcano? *(The baking soda reacted with the vinegar and created a gas that forced the lava out.)*
- If you tried this experiment more than once: Which experiment worked the best and why?

God created the earth and everything in it—including volcanoes. Some volcanoes are still active. If they erupt, the lava could destroy houses or villages too close to the volcano. God didn't make a mistake when He created volcanoes. There were no accidents when God created the world and everything in it. Everything He created was good and well-planned. We can confidently trust Him and His plans for us!

- What plans have you made that turned out well?
- What plans did you make that didn't turn out well?
- Jeremiah 29:11 tells us that God has good plans for us. What kinds of good plans could God have for you?

WHIRLYBIRD FLIERS

Try to create a "bird" that flies!

Bible Basis: Genesis 1:20-25

MEMORY VERSE:
How many are your works, O Lord! In wisdom you made them all; the earth is full of your creatures.
Psalm 104:24

BIBLE BACKGROUND

Often people gaze at creation and marvel that God created such an astonishing world for them to enjoy. Did God create things just for us? Each part of God's creation serves a purpose—to praise God. "The heavens declare the glory of God; the skies proclaim the work of his hands" (Ps. 19:1).

What about animals? It's hard to imagine a world without creatures that provide companionship, work, food, and entertainment. While animals give people pleasure and help, the Bible mentions sea creatures, wild animals, cattle, small creatures, and flying birds of the earth in the list of those praising God (Ps. 148:7, 10).

Some world religions look at the creation and worship it. Scripture warns people to worship the Creator and not the creation (Rom. 1:25). Whenever you gaze in awe at creation, let it be a reminder of God's power and majesty and lead you to worship Him.

You can prompt your students to respond with awe and praise to the Creator as well. What a wonderful opportunity to help children explore the wonders of God's creation and remember their Creator while they're young (Eccl. 12:1).

Teacher Tips:

This activity works best in an area where children can drop their birds from a high place and watch them flutter downward. If you have an open stairway, let the kids drop or throw them upwards into the center of the area. An indoor balcony would also be a good area to launch the whirlybirds.

When dropping the birds, let two students at a time drop their birds. Too many birds dropped at once will hit each other and not give good results.

Variations to the Experiment:

Let kids experiment with different types of paper: cardboard, cardstock, newspaper, tissue paper, construction paper, and printer paper. Extra paper clips and staples can be used to explore how weight affects flight.

Set out stickers or markers to decorate the birds. Encourage children to experiment with making birds of different sizes and different wing lengths.

Materials List:

- ❍ Paper (1 sheet for each child) Optional: different paper sizes and thicknesses
- ❍ Scissors (1 for each child)
- ❍ Pencil (1 for each child)
- ❍ Paper clips and/or stapler
- ❍ Markers and stickers

INVESTIGATION

1. Give each child the same size of paper (start with half a sheet of paper).
2. Have the children fold the paper in half. Using scissors, make two cut marks along the fold line starting at each edge (each cut about an inch and a half long).
3. After making the cut marks, unfold the paper so that it's in the original flat position. Form a handle out of the lower section of the paper by folding the two sides toward the back, leaving the middle third-section to become the handle. Keep the handle from opening while flying by using a paper clip on the bottom or stapling it. (Students will want to experiment with the effects of the weight from the paper clip and staples.)
4. Each child can decide what kind of a cut to make (straight, zigzag, curved, or their own style) from the top of the paper down to the fold line. The cut will affect how the whirlybird flies. After cutting, have the children fold one wing forward and the other wing backward.
5. Have each child write his or her name on the bird. Let the children decorate them.
6. Take the whirlybirds to an area to drop or throw them. Have the children hold them by the handle or the paper clip and then drop or throw them as high and far as they can. Watch to see which bird designs work best.
7. If you have time, let the children experiment and try to improve on their whirlybird designs, based on what they observed from the first flying session.

WHY DOES IT WORK?

Gravity pulls the whirlybird down through the air. However, molecules of air must move out of the way to allow the wings to continue downward. The air moves out of the way on the path of least resistance. Of course, some papers you use might not be strong enough to resist that slight pressure from the air and may bend upward, allowing the bird to drop faster and possibly in a different pattern. The angle of the paper wings in part determines the path of least resistance. If that path is the same direction for both wings, the bird will fly forward in a line. If the paths are in opposite directions, the bird will likely spin or descend in a more random path, depending on differences in the direction and force of the opposing paths the air follows.

END WITH A BANG

- Which wing design cuts worked best?
- Why do you think these worked best? *(The best wing lengths held lots of air under them.)*
- What would you try differently on your next bird design?
- What might affect flying conditions and change the results? *(air currents, a higher or lower dropping area, too many birds dropped at once, etc.)*

It was fun designing a bird! God designed real birds, and He made them perfectly the first time. Over the past century, people studied birds to learn how to create airplanes.

- Why do you think God created so many different kinds of birds?
- God's creativity shows in every bird and animal that He created. What's your favorite bird or animal, and how does it show God's creative design?

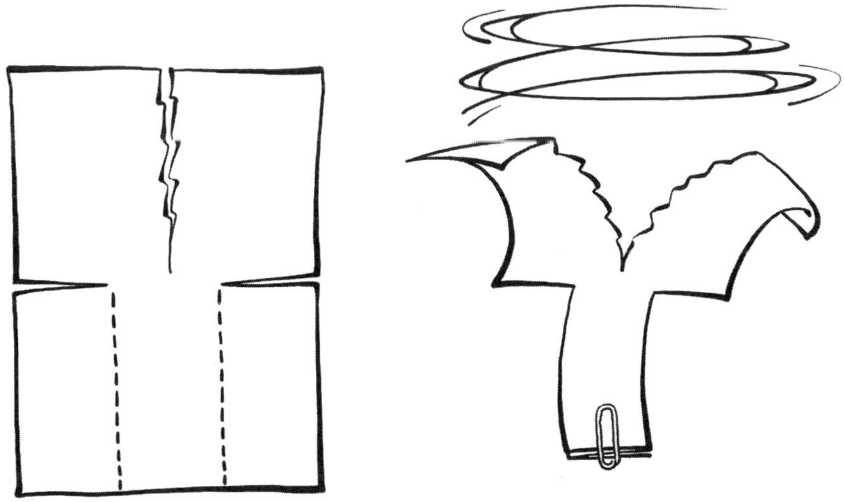

VANISHING ACT

The consequences of sin become visible in this experiment.

Bible Basis: Genesis 2:15-17; 3:1-24

MEMORY VERSE:
Blessed is the man whom God corrects; so do not despise the discipline of the Almighty.
Job 5:17

BIBLE BACKGROUND

God placed Adam and Eve in the Garden of Eden, a place with a name that means "paradise." The Bible refers to four rivers that flow from a single river of Eden (Gen. 2:10–14). The Tigris and Euphrates rivers are located in modern-day southern Iraq. One of the rivers was in Cush, most likely located in Africa, which leads to speculation that the Garden of Eden may have covered the whole Middle East.

God directly told Adam to not eat the fruit of the tree of the knowledge of good and evil (Gen. 2:16–17). Satan, disguised as a serpent, planted questions and doubts in the mind of Eve. Adam and Eve disobeyed, placing their own will above God's. Their choice immediately and directly impacted the delightful life they had enjoyed in the garden. Like we often do, they soon discovered that the results of their sin reached further than they may have anticipated.

Adam and Eve experienced a variety of consequences as a result of giving in to temptation and eating the fruit. They gained the moral independence they wanted, but at an enormous cost: hard work, painful childbirth, and physical death, in addition to severe spiritual consequences. Praise God that He provided a way of reconciliation through Christ so we may enjoy a restored relationship with God (2 Cor. 5:18)!

Teacher Tips:

The two brand-name chalks listed contain 95% calcium carbonate. Other chalks are synthetic and lack sufficient calcium carbonate to dissolve. You can find the recommended chalks at office supply stores or art and craft stores.

If you're unable to locate the suggested chalk, regular chalk will fizz for a minute, but won't dissolve. Even so, you can still get the point across as the children see the bubbles that are eating away at the chalk like sin eats away at our relationship with God.

Another alternative to chalk is to use the small, square pastel after-dinner mints. These dissolve completely in about five minutes. The chalk is more impressive because the kids can feel how hard the chalk is before the experiment.

Use vinegar with the highest percentage of acidity. The higher the acidity, the faster the chalk will dissolve.

Since liquids are used, you may want to cover the work area with newspapers or a plastic tablecloth.

Variations to the Experiment:

Try a variety of items to see what else dissolves in vinegar: chalks (sidewalk and regular chalk), gummy bears, mints, gumdrops, etc.

As you test the different liquids, make a chart that the students can fill in with the results of each experiment.

Materials List:

- ❍ Chalk: Crayola® Anti-Dust® or Prang® Hygieia® (both 95% calcium carbonate)
- ❍ Chalkboard
- ❍ 1–2 c. white vinegar
- ❍ Clear cups or jars (1 per liquid)
- ❍ Variety of liquids: orange juice, milk, water, soda, lemon juice, hydrogen peroxide, cooking oil, liquid dish soap, etc.
- ❍ Newspaper or plastic tablecloth

INVESTIGATION

1. Use chalk to write on the board "Sin has consequences." Pass the chalk around so each child can feel the "hardness" of the chalk, as you ask all to share ideas about the potential consequences of sin.
2. Explain that one consequence of sin is that it eats away at our relationship with God. Pour vinegar into a cup and add a piece of chalk. Note: The chalk will bubble as the vinegar dissolves it; within five minutes or less you should remove the chalk and show how much has been eaten away by the vinegar.
3. Try to write on the chalkboard with the dissolving chalk and ask kids to observe what's happening (it won't write).
4. Tell the class that it's their turn to experiment with other liquids that will eat away at the chalk. Set out the clear empty containers.
5. Choose a child to carefully pour one substance into the cup and drop in a piece of chalk. Depending on the number of liquids you're testing, break the chalk and just put a small piece in each cup.
6. Continue letting children choose a liquid to pour in a cup to test. Consider having them test the various liquids all at once, if time is a consideration.

WHY DOES IT WORK?

Chalk is composed primarily of calcium carbonate (CaCO3). The acid in the vinegar reacts with the chalk, causing carbon dioxide gas to bubble on the chalk. Bits of chalk break off and leave holes in the chalk.

This experiment also shows the effects of acid rain on statues or buildings made of limestone or other stones containing calcium carbonate.

END WITH A BANG

- **What surprised you the most about this experiment?**
- **Why does chalk dissolve in vinegar?** *(The acid in the vinegar eats away at the calcium in the chalk.)*
- **Why didn't the chalk dissolve in other substances?** *(Some liquids didn't have acids strong enough to dissolve the chalk.) Note: If you tested soda, you probably found that it did slightly dissolve the chalk because of the carbon dioxide.*

The chalk in our experiment suffered greatly when it went into the vinegar. Adam and Eve were like the chalk, and suffered greatly by eating the forbidden fruit. Their disobedience caused their relationship with God to break down, just like the vinegar broke down the chalk.

- **What are the consequences or results of sin?** *(The consequences of sin break down our relationship with God. Sin separates us from God.)*
- **Why does God sometimes correct or discipline us?** *(He wants us to learn to do what is right and not what is wrong.)*
- **How does God's correction or discipline show us that He loves us?** *(He loves us enough to care whether we choose right or wrong.)*

WATER WHEELIES

The paddle wheel keeps going to inspire us to keep doing what's right.

Bible Basis: Genesis 6:9–7:24

MEMORY VERSE:
Never tire of doing what is right.
2 Thessalonians 3:1

BIBLE BACKGROUND

The story of Noah and the ark recounts tremendous obedience on the part of God's faithful servant Noah. Several hundred years after Adam and Eve lived, the world was filled with people who had turned away from God. Yet one man and his family continued to follow God, even as God told Noah to prepare for a massive flood and gather two of every kind of creature.

Noah's faith in God propelled him to obey God's instructions and build a structure larger than an American football field, with a height of three stories. Imagine the job: being a first-time builder on an enormous project—without help from an expert at a home improvement store or access to a Web site! God revealed His step-by-step plan to Noah (Gen. 6:14–16) and the result was a floating vessel that endured the Flood.

It's much easier to show faith in God for a few minutes during a church service than to display faith that requires days, months, or years until the results are seen. The great faith chapter of Hebrews 11 notes that Noah's faith led him to obey God even when he didn't see any storms. Noah can be your example of not tiring as you faithfully serve God—especially in your role with your students.

Teacher Tips:

If you have access to a large kitchen sink, bathtub, or water basin, the paddle-boats will have a longer paddling time. If you have a small pan of water, one child at a time can launch a boat, using a finger or pencil to steer the boat away from the edge and keep the paddle turning longer.

Have fun with a nautical theme and inspire the children to give their boats names such as S.S. Joyful or Sea Serpent.

If you have a large group, two children can launch their boats simultaneously from opposite ends.

Variations to the Experiment:

Let the children experiment by making boats out of cardboard, paper plates, and other materials. Also have the children experiment with different-size proportions for the paddle, the boat, and the angle of the boat's bow.

Have one child wind the paddle clockwise and the other child wind the paddle counterclockwise. Watch one go forward and one go backward.

Materials List:

- ❍ Container of water at least 4" deep

For each child:

- ❍ Foam plate
- ❍ Large rubber band
- ❍ Scissors
- ❍ Crayons
- ❍ Ruler
- ❍ Pencil
- ❍ Optional: cardboard, paper plate, and other materials

INVESTIGATION

1. Cut a four-inch square from the plate and cut an angle into two edges to look like the front of a boat, or bow (rhymes with "how").
2. Create the opening for the paddle by cutting a one and a half-inch by two-inch piece on the opposite end (the stern). Trim the cut piece about a quarter of an inch. Save the piece that was cut; it will be the paddle.
3. Let the children decorate or write names on their boats with crayons.
4. Loop a rubber band over the end with the cut opening.
5. Insert the paddle between the sides of the rubber band and twist it several times. This winds up the paddle.
6. Release the boat in the water and watch the paddle turn as it powers the vessel.

WHY DOES IT WORK?

This experiment demonstrates two principles. Elastic potential energy is the energy stored in the twisted rubber band. When this energy is released, it turns into kinetic energy. If the rubber band is still wound up but the boat isn't moving, something has caused friction and there isn't enough potential energy to overcome the friction (such as hitting against the edge of the water tank).

The boat moves through the water because of Newton's Third Law, the Law of Action and Reaction. When an object is pushed, it pushes back with an equal and opposite force. As the paddle pushed against the water, the water pushing back against the paddle caused movement.

END WITH A BANG

- **What surprised you about the experiment?**
- **Why did the paddle keep turning?** *(Energy was stored in the twisted rubber band and then released.)*
- **Why did the paddle stop turning?** *(It stopped when all of the stored energy was released, or friction was encountered and not enough stored energy could push through the source of friction.)*

Just like the paddle wheel kept turning, we want to keep on doing the right things even when it gets tough or isn't fun. Noah worked and worked and he was rewarded for not giving up—the ark saved his family members' lives. God wants us to not get tired or bored of doing what He tells us to do.

- **When have you felt tired or bored of doing something you knew was good? Why did you keep on doing the right thing?**
- **How did you feel when you kept doing what was right?**

LEAD ON

Magnets make good leaders.

Bible Basis: Genesis 11:31–12:9; 17:1–8, 15; Hebrews 11:8

MEMORY VERSE:
Guide me in your truth and teach me, for you are God my Savior, and my hope is in you all day long.
Psalm 25:5

BIBLE BACKGROUND

After Noah and his sons, Shem, Ham, and Japheth, survived the Flood, God gave them the task of repopulating the earth (Gen. 9:1). Their descendants grew to occupy the known world. Hundreds of years later, God spoke to one of Shem's descendants, Abram.

Abram lived in Ur, a thriving commercial area, until God directed him to move. The first move, to Haran, was about 550 miles—quite an undertaking for a family during a time without cars and moving trucks.

During their time in Haran, Abram and his nephew Lot acquired people and possessions. God led Abram to move again, this time into the hostile territory of Canaan, and another 500 miles farther away from his original home.

Obeying God's leading isn't always easy, but God rewards faithful obedience. God changed Abram's name to Abraham and promised that he would be the father of many nations. Scripture records his faithfulness and God's reward of descendants as numerous as the stars and sand (Heb. 11:8–13). Today, God continues to lead His children and seek out those who will follow Him—no matter the cost. As you model obedience to God, may the children you teach recognize the joy that comes from faithfully following God and develop this lifelong habit.

Teacher Tips:

You may want to notify the children of this lesson ahead of time so they can bring in their own magnets. Try to have enough magnets for each child, or pair of children, to use. There are many different kinds of magnets with different strengths. Bring in a variety and watch how the filings react to each kind of magnet.

Iron filings will stick to magnets. Keep paper or a piece of clear acetate (overhead transparency material) between the magnet and the filings. Cover the work area with newspaper.

Hold the bottle of oil near a light to easily see the iron filings. If it's too hard to see the filings, you may want to add more to the oil. If they clump and settle quickly to the bottom, you may have too many. You can remove some by moving the magnet upward toward the bottle opening and then remove the filings with a plastic spoon or craft stick.

If you don't have iron filings, you can easily cut iron filings from clean steel wool by making tiny snippets about one-eighth of an inch long.

Remember to keep all magnets away from computers, audiotapes, and other magnetic devices—and share this warning with your students.

Variations to the Experiment:

If you have a magnet that will fit into the bottle, put the magnet into a clear plastic sandwich bag and hold the bag while submerging the magnet. Watch how the filings react to the magnet in the oil.

Let the children experiment with putting dry iron filings on a piece of transparency sheet. Hold a magnet below the sheet and watch the filings move. Set the transparency sheet with the filings on the table. Hold another transparency sheet above it with the magnet on top of this sheet. The filings will jump up to the underside of the upper sheet with the magnet.

Materials List:

- ❍ Bottle of baby oil
- ❍ Iron filings or steel wool cut into tiny snippets
- ❍ Magnets
- ❍ Plastic spoon or craft stick
- ❍ Optional: transparency sheets
- ❍ Optional: clear plastic drinking cup
- ❍ Water

INVESTIGATION

1. Peel the label off the baby oil bottle so the contents can be easily viewed.
2. Pour in a small spoonful of iron filings.
3. Screw the lid on securely and shake the bottle to disperse the iron filings. Bring a magnet near the bottle and watch the filings move. The iron filings will clump together if you hold the magnet closer than one-half inch.
4. Experiment by moving the magnet around faster, slower, closer, farther away, up, and down. If the filings clump together, shake the bottle to separate them or remove some with a plastic spoon or craft stick.
5. If you have enough magnets, let the children try their own experiments substituting water in a clear plastic drinking cup for the bottle of oil.

WHY DOES IT WORK?

Magnets have invisible magnetic fields around them. Each magnet has two poles: north and south. Each filing also has a north and south pole. Like or same poles repel or push away from each other, while opposite poles attract each other. The filings, attracted by the pole of the magnet, move through the oil. The iron filings line up around the opposite pole of the magnet and show the actual three-dimensional pattern of the magnetic field.

END WITH A BANG

- **Why did the iron filings move through the baby oil?** *(Each filing has a north and south pole. The filings move through the oil because they're attracted to the opposite pole of the magnet.)*
- **Which magnets worked best?**

The little bits of iron and metal followed the magnet. Wherever the magnet went, they followed. Abraham followed God just like iron filings follow a magnet. God led Abram in the right direction and God wants to lead you too.

- **How can people know what direction God wants them to go?** *(read the Bible, pray, listen for Him to speak to me, talk to other Christians, etc.)*
- **How do you feel when you follow God?**

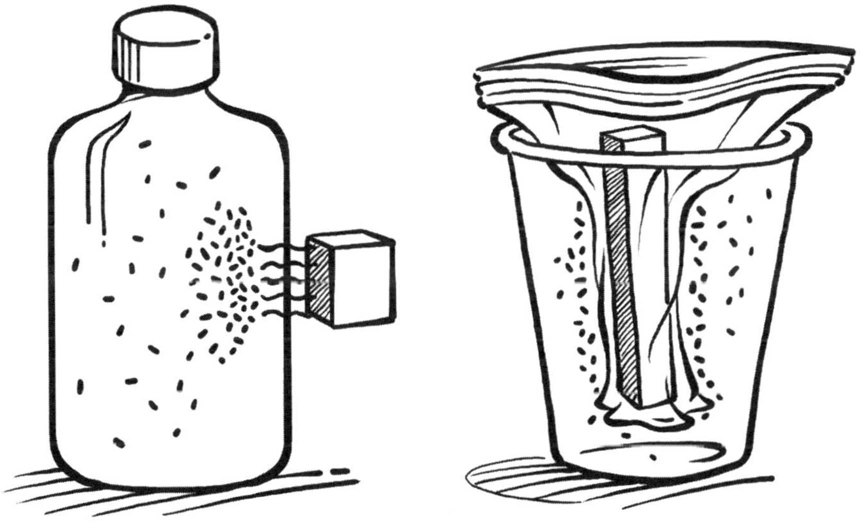

WEIRD AND WONDERFUL GOO

This substance does the impossible—it's both liquid and solid!

Bible Basis: Genesis 18:1-16; 21:1-6

MEMORY VERSE:
Nothing is impossible with God.
Luke 1:37

BIBLE BACKGROUND

Twice God promised Abraham that he would be the father to a great nation (Gen.12:1–3; 15:4–5). Abraham faithfully followed God and moved to Haran, and then on to Canaan, but he still didn't have an heir. Believing time had run out for him and his wife to become parents, he decided to "help" God by acting upon customs of the day that allowed a childless couple to adopt the son of a handmaid as a legal heir.

Abraham found out that despite his "help," God's plans are always fulfilled in God's ways (Prov. 19:21). Three men visited Abraham and his wife and said that one year later God would have fulfilled his promise and Sarah would have a son. These unrecognized visitors were the Lord Himself and two angels (Gen. 18:1, 10, 13, 33; 10:1). Twenty-five years after God issued the promise (Gen. 12:2–3), God fulfilled the initial promise through the birth of Isaac (Gen. 21:1–4).

Throughout the Bible we find testimony after testimony of God's faithfulness. God reminded Jeremiah that His covenant with the sun and moon couldn't be broken—neither could His covenant with Israel. Take comfort and refuge in knowing that God keeps all His promises.

Teacher Tips:

This gooey mixture will not stain, but even so, try to prevent getting the substance on clothing or the floor. Spread out newspapers or a plastic tablecloth on the work area. It helps to have a large bowl or plastic tub for each child or group of children. Use paint smocks if you have them.

Be aware that children will need to clean their hands after playing in the goo. Have wet wipes available or wash hands at a sink.

The mixture is so intriguing that the students will want to keep playing with it. You can send some home with each child in a plastic container or zip-top sandwich bag.

When finished with the experiment, don't pour the gooey substance down a drain. Instead, put any unwanted goo in a garbage bag for disposal.

Variations to the Experiment:

Let the children experiment with different proportions of cornstarch and water. Also, let the mixture sit for a few minutes and notice the change in its consistency.

After sitting a few minutes, stir the mixture and use it again and again. Check the difference between mixing the ingredients quickly and slowly. Place a small plastic toy or object on the surface. What happens?

Materials List:

- ❍ Newspaper or plastic tablecloth
- ❍ Strong stirring spoon
- ❍ Mixing bowl
- ❍ Measuring cups
- ❍ Large bowl or plastic tub (1 for each child or small group)
- ❍ Wet wipes

Goo Recipe:

To make a batch for a group of 4–6 children:

- ❍ 1½ c. cornstarch
- ❍ ½ c. water

Individual recipe:

- ❍ ¼ c. cornstarch
- ❍ 5 tsp. water

6 tsp

INVESTIGATION

1. Spread newspaper or a tablecloth over the work area. Measure cornstarch into the bowl and slowly add some of the water. Children should slowly mix the ingredients together with their hands. Keep adding water until the mixture is similar to the consistency of pancake batter. Adjust the mixture as needed. If the mixture is too wet, add a little more cornstarch. If the mixture is powdery, add a tiny bit of water. As the children manipulate the mixture, it will change consistency.
2. Have the children pick up a handful and squeeze it. When they stop squeezing, it will change from a solid to a liquid. Ask them to try to form the goo into a little pyramid in their hands, and then watch it melt away. Remind them to keep the mixture over the bowl or container.
3. Let the children experiment by putting their hands on the bottom of the mixture and quickly trying to remove their hands. Use a spoon to remove some of the goo and notice how it changes.
4. Bang on the substance with a spoon and watch it harden. Leave it alone and watch it turn back to liquid.

WHY DOES IT WORK?

The water and cornstarch goo mixture is called a suspension. A suspension sometimes works as one state of matter, then changes to act as a different state of matter, such as liquid to solid. Applying pressure on this suspension by simply pressing on it or squeezing it, causes the molecules in the suspension to line up and remain in a compacted alignment. They stay compacted as long as the pressure continues. That's why the suspension persists in behaving as a solid. As the amount of pressure decreases or completely subsides, the molecules move out of alignment, as if released from alignment to again move around more freely and randomly within the blob. Now the suspension behaves more like a liquid.

END WITH A BANG

- What surprised you the most about this experiment?
- What happened to the mixture when you kneaded or stirred it? *(The mixture turned solid.)*
- What happened to the mixture when it was left alone? *(It turned instantly back to liquid.)*

It seemed impossible for any substance to be both solid and liquid, but the goo was! Sometimes we might think something is impossible. Remember—nothing is impossible for God!

- God kept what seemed to be an impossible promise with Abraham. How do we know that God keeps His promises?
- Why do you think people forget that God can do what seems impossible?

CANDY BLAST OFF

God can burst through our problems like this candy blasts off.

Bible Basis: Genesis 24

MEMORY VERSE:
The righteous cry out, and the Lord hears them; he delivers them from all their troubles.
Psalm 34:17

BIBLE BACKGROUND

Abraham knew his son had an important role in fulfilling God's covenant. When it was time for Isaac to marry, Abraham and his family were living in Canaan. The Canaanites were known for their idolatry. Abraham wanted a wife for Isaac who would honor and worship the only living God. This task was impossible to fulfill in Canaan. To find a godly woman would require travel to where his family members, the Hebrews, lived. So Abraham sent a servant to make the 400-mile trek to Nahor. Most likely the servant was Eliezar of Damascus, who would have been Abram's heir before the birth of Isaac (Gen. 15:2).

God guided the servant as he prayed for help; even before his prayer was finished, Rebekah appeared (Gen. 24:12–15). Isaac was about 40 years old when he married Rebekah. His father would have been about 140 and we know that his mother Sarah died sometime after the marriage at the age of 127 (Gen. 23:1–2).

Today's Scripture passage reminds us that prayer is a powerful tool. God promises help to those who cry out to Him. As you cry out to God, watch for His answer to burst forth. Remember to thank the Lord for listening to your cries and delivering you from your troubles.

Teacher Tips:

Do this experiment outside since the soda leaves a sticky mess. If you're in a parking lot, be aware that wind might blow soda onto cars.

Either diet or regular soda will work; however, diet soda is less sticky when you're cleaning it up! The store brand of soda works as well, if not slightly better, than name brands.

Geysers can shoot several feet in the air when the candy is dropped into the bottle, so don't get your face directly over the bottle. Also, don't allow children to put in the candy as they may look into the bottle and wind up with a face full of soda.

Drop the candy into the bottle through a funnel or a piece of paper rolled to form a funnel. You can also check local teacher or toy stores for plastic tubing that can be inserted into the bottle that allows you to drop all the candy in at once. A tube forces the geyser much higher in the air.

Variations to the Experiment:

Have each child bring an unopened two-liter bottle of soda. Test and record the results of the different brands or types of soda to see which produced the highest geyser and the longest fountain (use a stopwatch).

Materials List:

- ❍ Mentos® mint candies (Note: Wintergreen Lifesavers® also work, but must be broken in half and might be harder to quickly insert into the bottle)
- ❍ One 2-liter bottle of diet soda
- ❍ Funnel or paper rolled to form a funnel
- ❍ Optional: stopwatch, plastic or vinyl tubing that fits securely over soda bottle opening

INVESTIGATION

1. Set an open bottle of diet soda on the ground and have the children stand back several feet.
2. Unwrap the Mentos® candy.
3. Use a funnel to drop an entire roll of candy into the soda. Do this very quickly. Once the geyser begins, you can't add more candy. The experiment only works once per bottle of soda.

Caution: Anticipate a strong and immediate geyser of soda, perhaps 10–15 feet. (Diet soda seems to generate more powerful geysers than regular and is also less sticky for cleanup.)

WHY DOES IT WORK?

The reaction is mostly a physical action more than a chemical reaction. The candy begins to dissolve immediately in the soda, releasing its gelatin and gum arabic ingredients into the soda. These two ingredients break the natural surface tension of water molecules in the soda, i.e. the tendency to attach to one another and hang on. Surface tension must break for the soda to come out, even a little bit, like when you just open the bottle. Normally, surface tension breaks more slowly so we can control the fizz. The candy escalates that because each piece has thousands of tiny pits. Each pit attracts a bubble of carbon dioxide (CO_2) gas. But the gelatin and gum arabic also break the surface tension of each bubble, allowing all the bubbles to expand very rapidly. All this cumulative and instant expansion throughout the soda creates the amazing soda blast.

END WITH A BANG

- **Why did the soda blast out of the bottle?** *(Pressurized carbon dioxide gas expanded instantaneously because the candy and its ingredients broke surface tension.)*
- **Which kind of soda made the biggest geyser?**
- **What would you try differently next time?**

In our experiment, the soda was stuck in the bottle. Sometimes we have problems and we can't seem to figure a way out of them. When we ask God, He will help us, just like the candy created and led the way for the soda to explode out of the bottle.

- **Are there any problems you feel stuck in?**
- **When have you asked God for help? What happened?**

CRAZY CAMERA

This camera tricks you and flips things upside-down!

Bible Basis: Genesis 25:27-34; 27:1-45

MEMORY VERSE:
Each of you must put off falsehood and speak truthfully to his neighbor.
Ephesians 4:25

BIBLE BACKGROUND

During Old Testament times, a birthright was an honor given to the firstborn son. It assured the boy of his inheritance and his role as family leader. The birthright was also useful to trace family lineages. The birthright in today's lesson had the added significance of being part of the line that would produce the Messiah.

Esau, the older of the twins, sold his birthright to his brother, Jacob. This wasn't deceptive or dishonest, but was a legally binding deal. Obtaining the blessing from his father placed Jacob in line for the covenant inheritance of Abraham. Jacob's descendants would become the 12 tribes of Israel, while Esau's descendants became the Edomites.

Jacob used trickery to get ahead instead of following God's way and trusting God for the blessing. Even today, Christians lose patience and often try to "help" God solve a situation. When we take things into our own hands, we rob God of the opportunity to work in our lives and produce the result He desires. We also rob ourselves of building our level of faith in Him.

Teacher Tips:

The Latin *camera obscura* means "dark room or chamber." The concept of the *camera obscura* has existed for centuries and was used in the 12th century to safely observe the sun and eclipses.

The waxed paper needs to be firmly taped in place to give a better image. Make sure the waxed paper is secured tightly before closing and taping up the box.

Using black and heavy tape will help keep the light out of the box. The darker the inside of the box, the better the image.

Variations to the Experiment:

Try a variety of sizes of boxes, sizes of holes, and distance of the paper from the hole.

Take the children outside to observe the trees and buildings upside-down.

Ahead of time, ask your students to each bring in a box to make their own cameras. You may want to have extra adult helpers for cutting the flap on the box, or have the children bring the box with the flap already cut. If time allows, they might enjoy covering the box with colorful paper or drawing on the box to decorate their cameras.

Materials List:

- ❍ Ruler
- ❍ Pencil or pen
- ❍ Scissors
- ❍ Empty cereal box (about 12" tall)
- ❍ Tape
- ❍ Waxed paper
- ❍ Pin
- ❍ Masking tape or wider tape
- ❍ Towel
- ❍ Optional: craft paint, markers, glitter pens

INVESTIGATION

1. On one side of the box, measure and mark a line five inches from the bottom of the box. Cut three of these edges of this side to form a flap.
2. Put the box on the waxed paper and trace the bottom of the box. Cut out the waxed paper piece. Open the flap on the box and securely tape the waxed paper piece about two inches from the bottom.
3. Carefully tape the flap closed so that no light enters the box.
4. Poke a pin into the center of the bottom of the box. You want a tiny hole. Note: A bigger hole may make the image appear out of focus.
5. Cut away the flaps on top of the box and cut a curve so the edges fit better against the forehead and face, just below the nose.
6. Have the child stand in a well-lit area. Choose another child to hold the camera against his face. Place a towel over the top of the camera and the child's head to reduce light entering the camera. Don't cover the viewing end (or pinhole end) of the camera. The child should see the other child's image upside-down on the waxed paper.

WHY DOES IT WORK?

As light reflected from the image comes through the hole, it converges. So, for example, light reflected from the top of the image (your friend's hair) traveled in a downward direction through the hole and kept going in a straight line to the bottom of the waxed paper. Thus, your friend appears upside-down. The waxed paper is semi-transparent. The opening in our eyes also converges images but our brains flip everything right-side-up. The box tricked your brain!

END WITH A BANG

- What did you expect to see?
- Why did the image appear upside-down? *(Light from the image converged as it came through the pinhole to the semi-transparent waxed paper.)*

In this experiment, the box tricked your brain. It projected the image upside-down. Jacob tricked his father and brother.

- Why does tricking someone, or not telling the truth, take away from our being like Jesus toward other people?
- How does being honest help us get along with others?

GEL BE GONE

Find out what ruins this fun gel just like jealousy ruins relationships.

Bible Basis: Genesis 37

MEMORY VERSE:
The fruit of the Spirit is love, joy, peace, patience, kindness, goodness, faithfulness, gentleness and self-control.
Galatians 5:22–23

BIBLE BACKGROUND

Families throughout history have faced the evil green-eyed monster of jealousy. Even people in the family line of the Messiah struggled with it. Jacob helped foster some of the jealousy between his sons by his obvious preference for Joseph, the son of his favorite wife Rachel.

Joseph only fueled the fire of jealousy when he told his brothers about his dreams. That resulted in more hatred that led to the brothers' conspiracy to get rid of Joseph.

Jealousy spoils the fruit of the Spirit in a Christian's life. That's why Paul warned the Corinthian believers to grow up and stop acting immaturely with displays of jealousy and quarreling (1 Cor. 3:1–4). Jealousy harms our relationships with God and with others. Fortunately, when we refuse to allow jealousy into our lives, we make ourselves a place where the Holy Spirit can cultivate the fruits of the Spirit that bring help and healing to relationships.

Teacher Tips:

Because the gel is such fun to play with, kids may forget to keep it over the bowl, so place newspapers on the table or work area.

The powder from one large diaper (one tablespoon) makes enough gel for three children to share. You can divide up the powder. Add one teaspoon into each bowl and add no more than half a cup of water.

You can ask children to bring in a diaper or two if they have some at home.

Caution children not to rub or touch their faces while playing with the mixture. After the experiment, children should wash their hands.

Because the crystals swell in water, don't pour the mixture down the sink. Dispose of it in a trash bag.

Variations to the Experiment:

Put one teaspoon of the powder in each bowl. Add different amounts of water and compare which result is wetter or fluffier. After comparing the samples, add salt to each one and see if there's a difference in how quickly they liquefy.

Experiment by adding warm water to one batch and very cold water to the other batch. Let the children describe how each feels and note other differences.

Bring in different brands of diapers to see which are more absorbent.

Another alternative to try is a plant polymer that absorbs water (available at garden centers).

Materials List:

- ❍ Water
- ❍ Clear bowl
- ❍ Measuring cups
- ❍ Measuring spoon
- ❍ Large diapers
- ❍ Large zip-top bag
- ❍ Stirring spoon or craft stick
- ❍ Salt
- ❍ Extra diapers and paper cups or disposable bowls (for individual experiments)

INVESTIGATION

1. Carefully peel off the inside layers of a diaper. You'll find a fine powder at the bottom layer of the diaper. Carefully shake the powder into a large zip-top bag and include the layers. Close the bag and shake. The white crystals will settle to the bottom. Throw away the lining.
2. Put the crystals into a glass bowl, add one cup of water, and begin to stir.
3. Let the children feel and play with the gel. Remind them not to rub their eyes, noses, or faces. Talk about how fun the gel is to feel.
4. If you have enough supplies, let each child or small group of three children make some gel and have fun playing with it. Use paper cups or disposable bowls for the individual experiments.
5. Ask the children: **What happened to Joseph when his brothers became jealous of him?** *(Joseph's jealous brothers sold him as a slave.)* **Jealousy hurts our lives. The gel is fun to feel and play with. Let's see what happens when we add salt to our gel. Imagine that we're like the gel and the salt is like jealousy**.
6. Pour one-quarter of a cup of salt into the bowl with the gel and ask a volunteer to stir the mixture. Within a minute or two, the mixture will turn back to water. If the children have made their own gel, have them take a handful and hold it. Add salt to completely cover it and have the children mix it together and hold it. The mixture will begin to melt in their hands.
7. Be sure children thoroughly wash their hands after the experiment.

WHY DOES IT WORK?

Diapers contain sodium polyacrylate crystals that absorb an amazing amount of liquid by expanding many times their original size. They're tiny super sponges that scientists call hydrophilic polymers. That means they love to hold water.

Salt acts as a solvent that makes the crystals give back some of the water through osmosis, i.e. moving something through a semi-permeable membrane (the skin of each crystal) to balance the amounts (of salt and also water) on both sides. The polymers release some water and absorb some salt.

END WITH A BANG

- **Why did the powder turn to gel?** *(It absorbed water like a sponge and softened.)*
- **What did the gel feel like in your hands?**
- **What happened when salt was added to the gel?** *(Water came back out of the gel so it wasn't as big or squishy.)*

It was fun playing with the gel until the salt was added. Just like the salt ruined the fun you had with the gel, jealousy can ruin your relationships with others.

- **What kinds of things make you jealous of others?**
- **How can we keep from being jealous?** *(be happy with who we are, remember all the things we have, thank God for blessing us so much, etc.)*

OVERCOMING POWER

Will good overcome evil? This experiment reveals the truth.

Bible Basis: Genesis 41:14–47:12

MEMORY VERSE:
Do not be overcome by evil, but overcome evil with good.
Romans 12:21

BIBLE BACKGROUND

Thirteen years after Joseph's brothers sold him into slavery, he was elevated from a slave to second-in-command of all of Egypt. He had adopted Egyptian dress and language. When his brothers saw him a few years later, they didn't recognize him—but Joseph recognized them!

Who would have blamed Joseph for seeking revenge? But God never honors revenge and clearly states that vengeance belongs only to Him (Deut. 32:35; Rom. 12:19). Instead, Joseph listened, and watched his brothers show concern for their father and exhibit remorse for how they had treated him. When Joseph was finally reunited with his father, he gave his family, including the brothers who sold him into slavery, the land of Goshen, near the modern day city of Cairo.

Often people choose a form of disguised revenge, such as gossiping, refusing to help, or simply ignoring a person. Our actions need to be pleasing to the Lord (Ps. 19:14). Any act of revenge or getting even, no matter how small, fails to bring glory to God. With God's help, we can choose to do good to others and bring honor and glory to God.

Teacher Tips:

Choose a wide-mouth jar so children can easily reach inside it. If you want children to conduct their own experiments, ask them to bring in jars, such as clean peanut butter jars. Remove labels so the jars are clear.

If you don't have marshmallows, use play dough or clay to hold the thumbtack. Whenever you use a sharp instrument like a pin, clearly state the rules for using the object. You'll want to remind the children to not poke others, or the balloon, with the sharp items. Look for push pins that stick out on the end, instead of the flat kind. They'll be easier for the children to stick into the marshmallow or clay.

Variations to the Experiment:

Try a variety of sizes of containers and different types of paper.

See who can build up the most static on the balloon. You can gauge the static level on the balloon by the distance it is from the jar when the paper flies off. The farther away the balloon is the stronger the static electricity.

If you're doing this experiment at home, rubbing the balloon along the back of a pet will produce lots of static electricity, and dogs seem to really love it!

Materials List:

- ❍ Wide mouth clear jar
- ❍ Push pin
- ❍ Marshmallow, play dough, or clay
- ❍ Tissue paper
- ❍ Scissors
- ❍ Pen or permanent marker
- ❍ Balloon
- ❍ Optional: wool scarf

INVESTIGATION

1. Secure the push pin into the marshmallow or clay so the point is sticking outward. Carefully set the marshmallow or clay inside the bottom of the jar with the tack point up.
2. Cut a piece of tissue paper into a one-inch by half-inch rectangle. Fold the rectangle in half to make a long skinny piece. Write the word "Evil" on each half of the tissue paper. Carefully balance the paper on the point of the push pin. The paper should look like a tent and balance without touching or resting on the marshmallow.
3. Blow up the balloon and tie it closed. Write "Good" on the balloon with a permanent marker.
4. Remind the kids that when someone does something evil or mean, we shouldn't be mean back to them. Instead, the Bible tells us that doing something good will overpower evil.
5. Rub the balloon on your hair or the carpet to build up a static electric charge. If you have a wool scarf, you can rub the balloon against it to build up static electricity. Then move the balloon near the jar. Watch the little piece of paper fly off the push pin.

WHY DOES IT WORK?

Everything is made of atoms. The atoms have positively charged protons and negatively charged neutrons. When the balloon is rubbed, that side of the balloon becomes negatively charged. As the negatively charged side of the balloon approaches the tissue paper, it strongly attracts the positively charged part of the paper resulting in the paper moving off the pin.

END WITH A BANG

- Why did the paper move? *(The paper moved because the negative charge of the balloon attracted the positively charged paper.)*
- What would you try differently next time?

The negatively charged balloon attracted the positively charged paper causing "good" to overpower "evil." This happens to us when we choose to not get even or return a mean action to someone who was mean to us. We can get power to overcome by letting the Holy Spirit help us choose a good action to do.

- When have you seen someone return a mean action to someone who was mean? What happened?
- What might have happened if a good action was done instead of trying to get even?

HIDDEN MESSAGE

God's Word is alive and even hidden messages are revealed.

Bible Basis: Deuteronomy 5:1-7; 6:5-9; 28:1-14; 31:9-32:47; Hebrews 1:1

MEMORY VERSE:
I have not departed from your laws, for you yourself have taught me.
Psalm 119:102

BIBLE BACKGROUND

At the age of 120, Moses wrote down the law that God spoke to him for the people of Israel. Just before his death, Moses gave responsibility to the priests to enforce the laws and regularly read them to the people.

Before Moses died, he reminded the Israelites to keep God's laws. This massive entourage had been meandering in the wilderness of Moab for 40 years, not far from the Jordan River, which bordered the new homeland God had promised to them. Moses trusted in the power of God and wanted the Israelites to recognize the power of God's written word in their lives. He called for them to rededicate themselves to God. Then he closed by reciting the words of a song that recounted God's faithfulness and power.

Today we're inundated with messages blasting at us from our cell phones, computers, televisions, billboards, and through the mail. We tend to look at these messages as more "alive" than words written hundreds and thousands of years ago. Yet, the truth is God's Word is alive and active and speaks daily to anyone willing to listen (Heb. 4:12).

Teacher Tips:

You can use a premixed grape juice, but the concentrate (undiluted) gives a stronger contrast. If you use the frozen concentrate, bring in a pitcher to mix any leftovers with water to serve to the children.

To avoid grape juice stains on children's clothing, supply paint smocks.

Variations to the Experiment:

Try experimenting with different kinds and colors of paper. Some have a coated surface and may turn sticky. Experiment using other acidic liquids such as vinegar, orange juice, lemon juice, etc.

Typically, lemon juice is used to write a hidden message; then the message is revealed when heat reacts with the dried juice. Let children experiment with lemon juice and a blow dryer to reveal the message.

Use the baking soda mixture to write one word of the Bible memory verse on each index card. Give each child a card to find the hidden word. Let children put the cards in the correct order to read the verse.

Materials List:

- ❍ Grape juice concentrate (frozen can, undiluted)
- ❍ Small foam plates (2 for each child)
- ❍ Spoon
- ❍ Baking soda
- ❍ Water
- ❍ Construction paper
- ❍ Cotton swab
- ❍ Paintbrush
- ❍ Index cards
- ❍ Measuring spoon
- ❍ Juice pitcher
- ❍ Optional: paint smocks, blow dryer

INVESTIGATION

1. On a small plate, mix one teaspoon of baking soda with one teaspoon of water. On another plate, put a small amount of grape concentrate. You may want to have only one plate with grape concentrate and have the children bring their pictures to the one location to reveal their message.
2. Using the baking soda mixture, children will take the cotton swab to write a message or draw a picture on the paper. When finished, children should blow on the paper or wave it in the air to help it dry. After the picture has dried, wipe off any excess baking soda from the paper.
3. Challenge children to try to guess what is written or drawn on someone else's paper. Then have the children paint grape juice on the paper and watch as the message is revealed.

WHY DOES IT WORK?

The juice is acidic and baking soda is a base, or non-acidic. When the acid in the juice comes in contact with the base, an acid-base reaction occurs and the message is darkened or revealed.

END WITH A BANG

- **Why did the grape juice reveal the message?** *(The acid in the juice reacted with the base of the baking soda and the reaction caused the message to be revealed.)*
- **What would you try differently next time?**

When you first wrote the message on the paper, it didn't seem interesting, or like there was anything there. Sometimes people think the Bible was written so long ago, it can't speak to them or possibly be important now. As you put grape juice over the message though, it became very colorful and interesting. That's a picture of how God's Word is for us. If we take time to read God's Word and let it speak to us, we can see that it becomes very real and speaks directly to us and to what's happening in our lives.

- **You may not hear a voice speak out loud, so how does God speak through His Word?** *(I may feel really loved by God, it might seem like God is talking right to me through the verse, it might be the exact answer to my problems, etc.)*
- **When have you read a verse and been amazed by how it fit exactly with what you felt or what you needed to hear? Tell us about it.**

GET THE PICTURE?

Look closely—two separate pictures will become one.

Bible Basis: Matthew 1:18-25; Luke 1:26-38; John 1:1

MEMORY VERSE:
And he will be called Wonderful Counselor, Mighty God, Everlasting Father, Prince of Peace.
Isaiah 9:6

BIBLE BACKGROUND

The marriage between Mary and Joseph would have taken place in two stages. Betrothal was the period when the man and woman didn't live together, but were legally bound to one another. The betrothal ceremony took place in front of witnesses. To break the betrothal would require a bill of divorcement. The betrothal time allowed the groom to fulfill his obligations of the financial terms of the marriage agreement. This time period ended with the wedding procession as the bride was brought to her husband and the families enjoyed a wedding supper.

After finding that Mary was pregnant, Joseph could have accused her of unfaithfulness, an act punishable by death. Although it would have been understandable to doubt that a virgin could have a child, Joseph believed the angel's message that was delivered through a dream. Isaiah had prophesied that Jesus would be born to a virgin (Isa. 7:14), a prophecy that was fulfilled when Jesus was born to Mary.

Our minds may have difficulty comprehending how Jesus was both human and divine. Think about some of the technological processes we accept without fully comprehending them: electricity, computers, lasers, the Internet. The essential foundational tenet of Christianity regarding Jesus simply requires faith. Thankfully, we don't have to explain it; we only need to accept that it did happen. Praise God for sending His Son into the world in human form to fulfill what none of us could accomplish.

Teacher Tips:

Place a dot in the center of each card to aid the children with their drawings. You may want to make a one-inch wide horizontal line on each card to help students perfectly line up the drawings. The line will mark the bottom of the person's top half and the top of the person's bottom half.

The picture doesn't have to be elaborate; a stick figure will work fine. Have the children use colorful markers or crayons to draw in the hair and clothing.

You could make up a stencil of a body outline. Put a line across the middle to remind the children to only use half of the picture on each card.

The children will want to keep their pictures, so use straws. If you have enough extra pencils, these are sturdier and are easier to turn.

Variations to the Experiment:

Children could draw other pictures that could combine to make a whole, such as a cage and a bird, a car and an open garage, a plate and food, etc.

Materials List:

- ❍ Index cards (2 for each child)
- ❍ Drinking straw or pencil (1 for each child)
- ❍ Crayons or markers
- ❍ Tape

INVESTIGATION

1. Give each child two index cards and a straw or pencil. Have the children turn the cards the tall way so the short end is closest to them.
2. On one card, have the children draw the top half of their person. Carefully lining up the picture, children will draw the bottom half of their person on the other card.
3. Set out crayons and markers so the children can color their pictures. They shouldn't add anything else to the background of the picture.
4. Tape the straw or pencil to the back of the card with the bottom half of a person drawn on it. If using a bendable straw, tape the flexible part to the card to hold it firm and straight.
5. Then tape the card with the top half so it covers the pencil (a picture shows on each side). Tape the back-to-back index cards along the top and the edges.
6. Remind children that Jesus had two parts because He was both God and human.
7. Show children how to hold the pencil between their hands and rub their hands back and forth to turn the picture. Although incomplete, the two pictures will appear together in the center.

WHY DOES IT WORK?

The brain holds onto the image, even as the image briefly disappears when the card is turned. The pictures overlap so they appear to combine and make a new picture. This is called persistence of vision. Animation uses this technique to make a still picture move.

END WITH A BANG

- **Why did you see one picture instead of two?** *(Your brain remembers the images and puts them together.)*
- **What would happen if you used more than two pictures?** *(Animation takes place when several pictures are shown quickly, so the object appears to move.)*

Just like your mind put the two separate pictures together to make a whole picture, Jesus had two separate parts—God and human. No one else in all of history is both God and man.

- **What makes Jesus different from any other person?** *(When He was on earth, He was both God and man.)*
- **Why was it important for Jesus to experience human things?** *(He knows what we experience and how we feel.)*

WAVE WATCHER

Don't give in to fear; ride out the storm with the Master of the waves.

Bible Basis: Mark 4:1-2a, 35-41

MEMORY VERSE:
I can do everything through him who gives me strength.
Philippians 4:13

BIBLE BACKGROUND

The Sea of Galilee may have looked peaceful when Jesus and His disciples set off in the boat, but this body of water is known for its sudden and severe storms. As cool air flows from the Mediterranean Sea through the mountain passes, it mixes with the warmer air trapped above the lake, resulting in violent storms that form quickly.

The fishermen with Jesus weren't alone on the lake. Mark wrote that other boats were out on the water at the same time (Mark 4:36). Fear was present in all the people in those boats, including the boat with Jesus' disciples. Although the disciples had seen Jesus perform miracles, their outbursts of fear demonstrated that their faith was still small and immature.

When Jesus spoke to the storm, it immediately quieted. Imagine the shock and relief of all the fishermen. Maybe you've responded with shock or surprise to Jesus' answer to your cries for help. No matter how big your storm in life may seem, Jesus can and will give strength and help.

Teacher Tips:

If you have a small group, bring enough supplies for each child to make a wave bottle to take home.

Colored plastic beads (from a craft store) will give children an idea of how boats might have bobbed up and down with the waves. Be sure the beads are distributed before the lid is sealed.

The oil can be messy, so cover the work area with newspaper. You can use duct tape to secure the lids of the bottles.

Variations to the Experiment:

Try other liquids to make a wave bottle. Experiment with filling a bottle two-thirds full with water and add blue food coloring. Fill the remainder of the bottle with baby oil. Discuss the similarities and differences between this wave bottle and the one filled with vinegar and oil.

Materials List:

- ❍ 16 oz. or 2-liter clear bottle (remove the label)
- ❍ White vinegar
- ❍ Blue food coloring
- ❍ Cooking oil
- ❍ Plastic bead
- ❍ Duct tape
- ❍ Newspapers

INVESTIGATION

1. Fill the plastic bottle one-third full of white vinegar. Add one drop of food coloring and shake the bottle until the vinegar turns blue.
2. Completely fill the rest of the bottle with cooking oil. Drop a bead into the water. Secure the lid tightly.
3. Gently tip the bottle back and forth and watch the waves crash against the bottle. The bead floats on the wave.

WHY DOES IT WORK?

The vinegar is denser than the oil. The two will not mix. The oil will stay above the vinegar even when the bottle tilts. Liquids that are of different densities often will not mix. This phenomenon demonstrates immiscible liquids, or liquids that don't mix.

END WITH A BANG

- Have you seen real waves on a lake or ocean? Did our experiment look like real waves?
- Why did the oil float on top? *(The oil is less dense than the vinegar.)*
- What would you try differently next time?

When the bottle tilts back and forth, the waves crash against the bottle. In nature, storms can be very strong and last for a long time. The men on the boat with Jesus were afraid, but Jesus told the storm to stop—and it obeyed Him!

- When have you been afraid?
- How can Jesus help you when you're afraid?

COLOSSAL CANDY CONSTRUCTION

Little gumdrops gather into an impressive structure.

Bible Basis: Luke 1:1-4; John 4:42; 20:28-31; Matthew 26:63-64; Mark 8:27-30

MEMORY VERSE:
These are written that you may believe that Jesus is the Christ, the Son of God.
John 20:31

BIBLE BACKGROUND

The Old Testament explained the need for a Deliverer and set the scene for the appearance of the Messiah. Each of the first four books of the New Testament paints a picture of Christ's life on earth. The accounts are told through the particular backgrounds or perspectives of each writer.

Matthew is full of messianic language, references many Old Testament verses, and was written with a Jewish audience in mind. Mark's record is a chronological look at Jesus' life. Mark traveled with Paul on a missionary journey and his writings reflect a desire for Romans to see Jesus as God's Son. Luke was a Greek doctor and detailed more illnesses and miracles relating to healing. John focused on the audience of new believers or seekers who had not yet claimed Christ as their Savior. He called himself "the disciple whom Jesus loved" (John 21:20). Jesus called John and his brother, James, "Sons of Thunder" (Mark 3:17).

When educators want to teach a concept, they often use different teaching styles to reach students' learning styles. Praise God that the important message of the good news of Christ was given to us in four different messages that work together to tell the story of salvation. Take time to pray for your students to be open to receive that message and act upon it.

Teacher Tips:

Buy an extra bag of gumdrops so the children can eat some while they work. You can use mini-marshmallows, but they aren't as strong as the gumdrops. The gumdrops leave sugar everywhere, so cover the area with newspapers or build the structures outdoors. Note: Check with parents for any allergies children may have.

Children will enjoy building and rebuilding. Gumdrops can be reused. Remind children not to eat candy that has been touched by others.

Supply plenty of toothpicks for connecting the structures.

Be sensitive to children who may be ready to have the salvation message explained, and be prepared to pray with them.

Variations to the Experiment:

If you have a large group, children can work in teams of four to six who put their individually-made section pieces together to form a structure. Compare the different structures to see which was the tallest, the best design, or the most unusual structure.

After completing the group structure, let the children experiment with building using different shapes. You may want to direct children to build a structure using only squares, and another structure using only triangles. Which shape is stronger?

Test the strength of the structures by placing a book or other object on top of them.

Materials List:

Per group of 4 to 6 students:

- ❍ Bag of gumdrops (9 oz.)
- ❍ Box of toothpicks

INVESTIGATION

1. Have the children sort the gumdrops by color. Give each child a few gumdrops of the same color. Children will be able to easily identify their sections if they build using only one color.
2. Use toothpicks to connect the gumdrops into a shape or design that will be hooked together with other students' designs to form one big gumdrop structure. Children can use as few as three gumdrops or as many as eight.
3. Choose a child to set his or her section as the base of the structure. One at a time, direct each child to add his or her section to the base by using toothpicks. The structure may need to be built wider if it appears too weak to hold any more height.
4. If several groups made structures, award a special title to each structure such as highest, widest, most unusual, prettiest, sturdiest, best designed, etc.

WHY DOES IT WORK?

Structures stand or fall as forces push (compression) or pull (tension) on its parts. The triangle shape is one of the strongest shapes and is commonly seen on bridges. The shape works because as compression forces push down on its top peak, trying to make it collapse, tension forces from the triangle's base pull and hold the sides up, keeping it all together. The three sides work together to hold each other in place. A square is a weak shape. When pressure is applied, the gumdrop joints are the weakest point and allow the structure to fold.

END WITH A BANG

- **Which shape makes the stronger structures?** *(Triangles are stronger than squares.)*
- **Why were some structures able to be built higher?** *(They have a better base or use triangles.)*
- **What can happen to the sections that used squares?** *(They can fold and collapse because the gumdrop joints are a weak point.)*

Each child's gumdrop structure is like a book of the Bible. The gumdrop structures are unique and each one is interesting and well-planned. When put together, they form a cool structure that shows off its many independent sections. The Bible consists of 66 books that could stand alone but when joined together, they give a complete picture of Jesus!

- **How does the Old Testament tell about Jesus?** *(The promises of a Savior all point to Jesus.)*
- **Why is it important that the whole Bible tells about Jesus the Savior?** *(People need to understand that only Jesus can forgive and save them from their sins.)*

REJOICIN' RAISINS AND GLAD GRAPES

These grapes and raisins can't stand still—they have good news to celebrate!

Bible Basis: Luke 2:21-38

MEMORY VERSE:
To all who received him, to those who believed in his name, he gave the right to become children of God.
John 1:12

BIBLE BACKGROUND

Mary and Joseph followed Jewish law and had Jesus circumcised eight days after He was born. By Jewish law, a mother underwent a 40-day period of purification after the birth of a son. At the end of the 40 days, Mary and Joseph took Jesus to the temple in Jerusalem, about five miles from Bethlehem.

Normally, a lamb would have been sacrificed at the temple. Mary and Joseph were poor and brought the sacrifice of doves or pigeons, allowed by Jewish law for anyone who couldn't afford a lamb.

While in the temple, two people recognized the baby as the long-awaited Messiah. Simeon held and blessed the One who would provide salvation. Anna also recognized the child as the Redeemer of Israel. Jewish law required two witnesses for something to be proven true. God brought these two people together at the exact moment to bear witness that Christ the Messiah had come.

Jesus' life was surrounded with fulfilled prophesies and amazing miracles. Not all who looked upon Jesus during His life received Him as their Savior. Jesus came to fulfill God's promise of a Savior—that's worth celebrating!

Teacher Tips:

You can use a two-liter bottle of ginger ale, but also bring an empty soda can for the static electricity part of the experiment.

Set out one glass full of water so the children can see the difference in results between water and the carbonated drink.

Variations to the Experiment:

Try several types of soda to see which are more carbonated. Clear sodas make it easier to see the raisins and grapes.

Test a variety of combinations of raisins and grapes in each glass.

Have children try a variety of other small items to see if they'll "dance" like the raisins and grapes. Try testing: different dried fruits, coins, marshmallows, beans, a piece of chocolate, etc. Before testing each item, ask the children to predict the result. Record the results for each item tried.

Materials List:

- ❍ Clear drinking glasses
- ❍ Ginger ale
- ❍ Raisins
- ❍ Grapes
- ❍ Empty soda can
- ❍ Balloon
- ❍ Optional: variety of other small items
- ❍ Optional: wool scarf

INVESTIGATION

1. Do this experiment on the floor in a large open area. Pour the soda into several glasses and place them on the floor in a large circle. Ask the children what they think will happen when a raisin or grape is dropped into the soda.
2. Arrange your group so each child or pair of children has a glass in front of them on the floor. Let each child or pair determine how many raisins or grapes will be put into their glass. Make sure each glass has a different combination.
3. As they're dropped in, explain how the grapes and raisins look like they're happy and dancing around, just like Simeon and Anna rejoiced when they knew the Messiah had come to earth.
4. Blow up and tie the balloon. Place the soda can on its side in the middle of the circle. Tell the group that the soda can represents Jesus coming to earth. Rub the balloon against your hair, a rug, or a wool scarf to build up static electricity. Remind children that Jesus came to save people from their sins and when people receive Jesus as their Savior, they rejoice! Hold the balloon so the side you rubbed is near the can. The can will roll toward the balloon. Use the balloon to lead the rolling soda can to one of the experiment glasses.
5. Let the child with that glass take the balloon and rub the balloon to build up more static electricity. Then the child should use the balloon in the same way you did to lead the soda can toward a different glass. Continue until the balloon has visited all of the glasses.

WHY DOES IT WORK?

Raisins/Grapes:

The irregular surface of raisins allows space for carbon dioxide gas to collect. The gas bubbles rise as they expand. When enough gas bubbles have collected on the raisin's surface, the raisins dance toward the surface. After the raisin reaches the surface, the gas is released into the air, causing the raisin to head downward to the bottom of the glass. As the raisin starts to gather more gas bubbles, it starts to rise again.

Soda Can Roll:

Rubbing the balloon on your hair or the rug charges it with electrons (electricity). The electrons on the balloon attract the protons on the soda can, causing it to roll. You can switch directions by moving the balloon to the other side of the can.

END WITH A BANG

- **What did you think would happen to the raisins and grapes?**
- **Which did you think would be more active in the glass?**
- **Why didn't the experiment work with the water?** *(The water wasn't carbonated or didn't produce carbon dioxide gas.)*
- **How long do you think the raisins and grapes would keep moving?** *(They will move as long as the carbonation remains, causing more carbon dioxide gas.)*
- **Why did the can roll when the balloon was near it?** *(The balloon built up electrons or electricity from rubbing, and the protons in the can moved to be near the electrons. Protons and electrons are attracted to each other.)*

Raisins and grapes can't really rejoice because they don't have feelings. Imagine how excited Simeon and Anna were to be in the temple on the day when baby Jesus was dedicated. They had waited their whole lives for that very moment. Jesus had chosen to come to earth to provide a way for people to go to heaven. What an amazing Savior!

- **How did both Simeon and Anna show that Jesus is the Savior that God promised?** *(They both said that Jesus was the long-awaited Savior.)*
- **How do you think you would have reacted if you had been in the temple when Jesus was dedicated?** *(happy, joyful, excited, surprised, confused, etc.)*

ICE CUBE TOWERS

Use wisdom to turn these ice cubes into a tall tower.

Bible Basis: Luke 2:41-52

MEMORY VERSE:
Remember your Creator in the days of your youth.
Ecclesiastes 12:1

BIBLE BACKGROUND

Jews attended three yearly feasts: Passover (commemorating the death angel passing over the homes of Israelites just before they left Egypt), Pentecost (a harvest festival), and the Feast of Tabernacles (commemorating the temporary housing used during the 40 years before the Israelites entered the Promised Land). The Passover was considered the most important of the feasts.

Since Jesus was now 12, the age when a Jewish male officially prepares to become a man and enter the religious community, it was important that He attend the Passover feast in Jerusalem. Jesus, His parents, their extended family, and others traveled 70 miles from Nazareth to Jerusalem.

While in Jerusalem, Jesus spent time with the religious leaders. Just think how amazed your pastor would be if a 12-year-old spoke theology with understanding and displayed astounding accuracy in answering doctrinal questions. Jesus amazed the religious leaders and showed His true identity by referring to the temple as His Father's house.

Even at a young age, Jesus set an example of growing in His knowledge of God. What a wonderful opportunity you have to help the children increase their knowledge of Jesus.

Teacher Tips:

Have towels handy to clean up melted ice cubes or for kids to warm their hands with after the experiment.

The more saltshakers used, the speedier the project will be.

Patience is needed, and a light touch is helpful. Remind kids to carefully place the ice cube on top and hold it in place without wiggling the cubes as they bond together.

Variations to the Experiment:

Try different shapes of ice cubes to see which ones work better and why. Ideas for other ice cubes: cylinder shapes that go into water bottles, round or novelty-shaped cubes, or cubes that have one flat side and one rounded side (like in some refrigerator door ice makers).

Try other compounds such as sugar to see if they melt the ice.

Have the children make an ice cube tower with a base of four cubes. Encourage teamwork to construct a tower.

Use a stopwatch to see how long it takes to melt an ice cube using only salt. Let kids make predictions before you start.

Bring in a plastic sandwich bag with sugar and a different bag with some salt. They'll look alike but only one will produce melting. Discuss how we can be fooled by outward appearances, but actions won't fool people—only salt melts the ice.

Materials List:

- ❍ Ice cubes (square, symmetrical)
- ❍ Salt shakers
- ❍ Bowl or foam plate (1 for each child)
- ❍ Large bowl to hold ice cubes
- ❍ Towels
- ❍ Optional: other ice cube shapes, sugar

INVESTIGATION

1. Set out a large bowl of ice cubes. Give each child a bowl or plate and challenge group members to see how tall an ice cube tower they can build. (Generally, two or three make the tallest tower that will stay together.)
2. Ask why they aren't able to keep building it higher. (The ice cubes are slippery and slide off each other.)
3. Set out the salt; ask the kids to figure out how the salt can help them build a tower. The child who figures out or answers that salt melts ice is correct and should demonstrate how it works.
4. Show that by sprinkling salt on an ice cube, the other cube placed on top of the first will refreeze and hold the two together. Prompt children to look carefully to observe the melting and refreezing.
5. Let the kids experiment with salt and the ice cubes.

WHY DOES IT WORK?

Temperature and the fine line between melting and freezing water make this experiment work. Water freezes at zero degrees Celsius, but ice also melts at zero degrees Celsius. There's a fine temperature line between the melting and freezing points, and it's difficult for most of us to maintain that exact temperature for any length of time. In this case, that works in our favor.

Salt prevents the water from refreezing because saltwater freezes at temperatures lower than zero degrees Celsius—how much lower than zero degrees Celsius depends on the amount of salt in the water. The more salt, the colder the temperature needs to be for the water to freeze.

However, the amount of salt in this experiment is limited, so as more ice melts, the water becomes less salty. Thus, the refreezing temperature rises closer to zero degrees Celsius. As the water refreezes and stays that way, your tower goes higher.

END WITH A BANG

- **Why weren't you able to build a tower very high at first?** *(The ice cubes kept sliding because they were slippery from melting.)*
- **How did the salt make it possible to build a taller tower?** *(The salt melted the ice and then refroze it, bonding it to the other ice cube.)*
- **How many ice cubes were you able to stack?**

At first we didn't know how to successfully build a tower, but then we learned that the secret to growing a stack of ice cubes into a tower is to add salt. Our knowledge produced results for us. When Jesus was a boy, He showed His knowledge of God in the temple. God is pleased when we learn about Him also!

- **How do we show that we know about God?** *(we learn Bible verses, tell what we've learned, answer questions, we encourage other Christians, we share Jesus with those who don't know Him, etc.)*
- **How can you grow in wisdom about God?** *(I read the Bible, listen to the pastor, talk with God, listen to Him, follow the examples of other Christians, etc.)*

EYE SPY

This periscope helps kids see up and around their problems.

Bible Basis: Luke 4:1-13; Hebrews 2:18; 4:15

MEMORY VERSE:
But when you are tempted, he will also provide a way out so that you can stand up under it.
1 Corinthians 10:13c

BIBLE BACKGROUND

Jesus' temptation most likely took place outside the city of Jericho. It was near the end of the 40-day fast when Satan began to tempt the Son of God. Satan seems to wait until his victims are at their weakest. The first temptation was to turn the stones into bread, something that would appeal to a body starved of food during a time of fasting. While this was something Jesus easily could have performed, it would have gone against God's will.

Jesus didn't argue with the tempter. Instead, He drew upon and effectively used the powerful weapon of Scripture. The first Scripture quoted, Deuteronomy 8:3, stated that man does not live by bread alone. Next, Jesus responded to Satan's plea to worship him by stating the command to worship only the Lord (Luke 4:8; Deut. 8:13). Lastly, Jesus quoted the admonition to not test the Lord (Deut. 6:16).

Even Satan quoted Scripture (Ps. 91:11–12). True to his form, Satan twisted God's words, just as he did in Genesis 3 when he spoke with Eve. However, in this situation, the power of God's Word prevailed and Satan left the scene of the temptation defeated. No wonder Paul told Christians to include the sword of the Spirit, the Word of God, as part of the armor needed to fight the enemy (Eph. 6:17).

Teacher Tips:

Bring extra handheld mirrors. The small compact or purse-size mirrors are great for the periscope, but larger handheld mirrors are better for experimenting.

Explain safety rules: don't run with the mirrors and don't shine light directly in another's eyes.

If you have a large class, make one or more periscopes ahead of time and bring them into the class.

If you have a small class, have each child take a turn helping cut and tape the periscope.

Variations to the Experiment:

Let children stand on one side of the wall near a doorway with another child on the other side. They can angle the mirrors to see around the corner.

Have children stand around the room at various distances and angles from each other and hold a mirror. The first child holds the mirror at an angle so his or her reflection can be seen and reflected to the second child's mirror. See if kids can figure out how to angle the mirrors to pass the first child's reflection through the mirrors to the last child. They may need to move to get a better position to pass on the reflection.

Experiment with making shorter or longer periscopes. Try a toilet paper roll, paper towel roll, or a wrapping paper roll. You could also use a box or cardboard folded and taped to make a periscope.

Materials List:

- ❍ Empty 1-quart milk or juice carton
- ❍ Scissors
- ❍ Strong tape
- ❍ 2 pocket-sized mirrors (not magnification mirrors)
- ❍ Optional: handheld mirrors for kids to use for experimenting

INVESTIGATION

To make the periscope:

1. Cut three sides of the top of a clean milk carton so the lid opens and bends, but is still attached.

2. Cut three sides of the carton's bottom, making sure the uncut side is on the opposite side from the uncut side of the lid.

3. Tape a mirror onto the inside of the lid and then tape a mirror onto the inside of the bottom of the carton. Note: You can tape handheld mirrors, but you'll need very strong tape so the mirrors don't fall out.

4. The mirrors on the flaps are moveable so you can create just the right angle (45 degrees) to make them reflect the image. Look in one end at the mirror and then adjust the mirrors so that you can see what's reflected through the mirror at the other end.

Experiments with the Periscope:

1. Explain that a periscope is used to see up and over objects or around things. It allows us to see things we normally couldn't see. Have a child hold a large paper or newspaper in front of his or her face while making a funny face. Choose a volunteer to look over the paper with the periscope to tell what kind of face the child is making. Let several children try this experiment.

2. Have one child sit under a table and use the periscope to see the other children sitting around the table. For fun, have each child hold up some fingers so the child under the table can check out how many fingers each child is holding up.

3. Choose one child to take the periscope and stand outside the door. Pick another student to stand just inside the doorway. When the child with the mirror sees and correctly identifies the other child, he should give the periscope to someone else to continue with the experiment until all the students have had an opportunity to use the periscope.

WHY DOES IT WORK?

You see an object because light bouncing off the object enters your eye. If the object is around a corner, the light can't bounce to your eye. The mirrors on the periscope are angled to reflect the light off the object onto your eye, so you can see it.

END WITH A BANG

- **When would you like to use a periscope?** *(to see what my friend is doing around the corner, to know when someone is coming to my room, to see over the fence, etc.)*
- **How does a periscope work?** *(The mirrors angle so they reflect and show what's around the corner or at a different angle.)*

Just like the periscope was used to be able to see around obstacles and show a way out, God gives us a special tool to help us. When Satan tempted Jesus, He used Scripture to provide a way out of the temptation. Sometimes we have problems and can't see our way out of them—God's Word is the perfect periscope to see beyond our problems.

- **How does knowing the Bible help you fight wrong?** *(By knowing what the Bible says and remembering to use it when we're tempted.)*
- **Why is the Bible like a periscope?** *(It helps us see a way out of our problems.)*

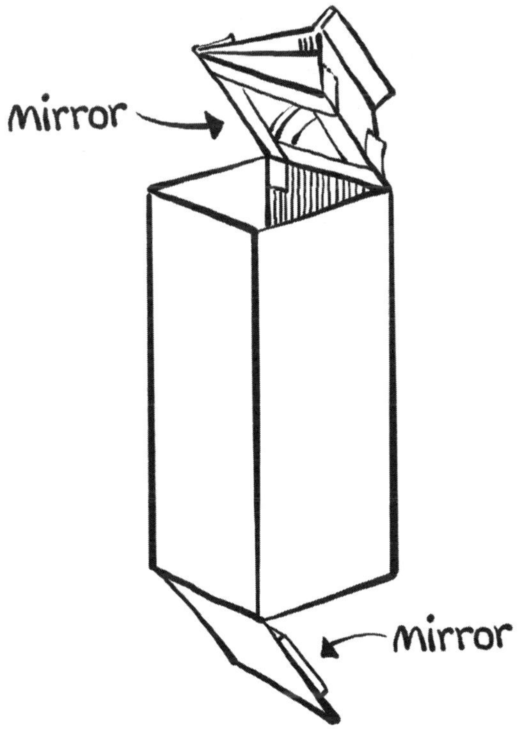

BREATHLESS BALLOON BLOW-UP

Can you blow up a balloon without touching it?

Bible Basis: Luke 7:1-10

MEMORY VERSE:
To him who is able to do immeasurably more than all we ask or imagine, according to his power that is at work within us.
Ephesians 3:20

BIBLE BACKGROUND

In New Testament times, Palestine was under Roman rule. The presence of Roman soldiers was a constant reminder that the Jews were not free. Most encounters between Jews and Roman soldiers were hostile.

Roman and Jewish customs and religious beliefs were very different and the Jews did not look upon the Romans with favor, most of the time. The centurion mentioned in this passage exhibited compassion for the Jews and helped them build a synagogue. This centurion had a humble and believing spirit that showed a remarkable understanding of Jesus' power. The centurion's faith amazed Jesus.

Jesus tells us if we have faith the size of a mustard seed we can see God do mighty things (Matt. 17:20; Luke 17:6). Praise God that He is willing to take our tiny faith and show us more than we could imagine (Eph. 3:20)!

Teacher Tips:

Balloons pop or leak, so always have extras.

Have someone hold the bottle after it's filled with vinegar so it doesn't tip and accidentally mix the solutions.

When the balloon starts to deflate, shake the bottle to re-fizz the vinegar and baking soda. The balloon should inflate again.

You can use duct tape to secure the balloon onto the bottle.

Children will want to do this experiment for themselves and may also want to take it home to show their families. Notify children ahead of time to bring in their own empty soda bottles.

Variations to the Experiment:

Try a variety of bottle and balloon sizes. If using a 16-oz. soda bottle, try a combination of six tablespoons of vinegar and three teaspoons of baking soda.

Materials List:

- 2-liter empty, plastic soda bottle (2qt.)
  1 liter = 1.06 qts
- One 12" balloon
- ⅓ c. baking soda
- 1 c. vinegar ½ c vinegar
- Toothpick
- Funnel
- Optional: duct tape

INVESTIGATION

1. Ask the kids to suggest ways to blow up the balloon without using their mouths to blow air into it.
2. Pour the vinegar into the bottle.
3. Put the baking soda into the balloon. A funnel helps, with a toothpick, to push the baking soda through the funnel.
4. Secure the balloon onto the bottle opening, being careful to not spill any baking soda into the bottle. You may want to tape the balloon onto the bottle. Let the balloon hang limply to the side.
5. Talk about how impossible the experiment seems since nothing is happening!
6. Then explain that when God is involved in our problems, we see His amazing power doing what we couldn't do.
7. Hold the balloon directly over the opening so the baking soda falls into the bottle. Shake the balloon to make certain all of the baking soda is released.
8. The mixture in the bottle will begin to bubble and the balloon will begin to inflate.

WHY DOES IT WORK?

The vinegar and baking soda combine to produce a chemical reaction that makes carbon dioxide gas. The balloon inflates due to the pressure of the gas formed in the bottle. The more pressure, the more the balloon inflates.

END WITH A BANG

- **How did the balloon inflate?** *(The baking soda and vinegar made a gas that filled up the balloon.)*
- **How long do you think the balloon will stay inflated?** *(Unless the air is released by a hole in the balloon, it will stay fully inflated for hours and then gradually lose air.)*
- **What would you try differently next time?**

Just like it seemed impossible for the balloon to be blown up without air, it seemed impossible that the Roman soldier's servant would live. But we can see from the Bible that no problem is too big for Jesus!

- **Why did the situation seem impossible to the Roman centurion?** *(The Roman soldier's servant was sick and he had faith that the only one who could heal him was Jesus, a Jew.)*
- **How did Jesus solve the centurion's big problem?** *(Jesus healed the man from a distance.)*

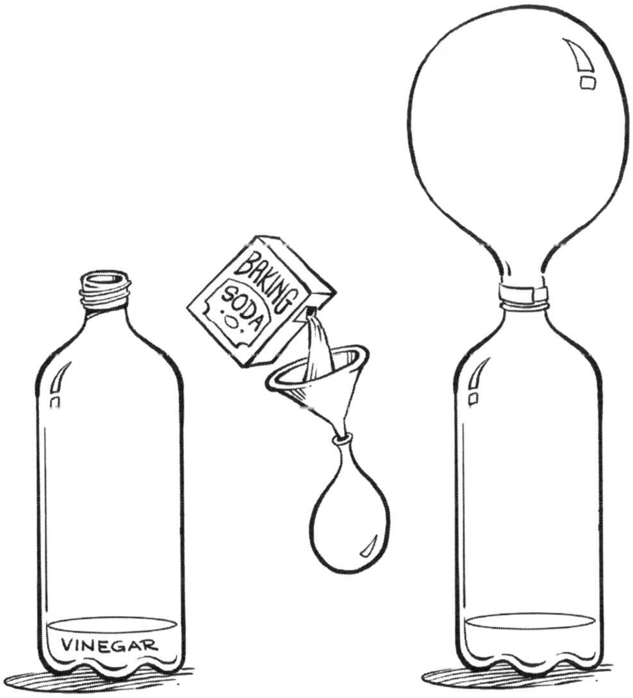

WATER WONDERS

Pushed away and pulled together—strange things happen in the water.

Bible Basis: Luke 19:1-10

MEMORY VERSE:
The Son of Man came to seek and to save what was lost.
Luke 19:10

BIBLE BACKGROUND

Throughout history, the working class has not appreciated tax collectors. In Jesus' day, Jewish tax collectors collected taxes for the Roman rulers of the land. Zacchaeus wasn't paid a salary by Rome, but he was allowed to collect extra money from the Jews.

Zacchaeus climbed a sycamore tree, which commonly lined the streets of Jericho. The sycamore tree mentioned in Luke 19:4 is different from the American sycamore. The biblical sycamore had soft wood and was an evergreen relative of the fig tree.

Zacchaeus demonstrated a total change when he encountered Jesus. His offer to pay four times the amount that he overcharged anyone showed his knowledge of Scriptures, since Moses set the penalty for stealing a sheep as a repayment of four sheep (Exod. 22:1). But it wasn't this action, or work, that brought salvation to Zacchaeus, rather the action, or work, was a result of a changed heart and life.

While the crowd displayed hostility and judged Zacchaeus, Christ accepted him and was able to see his repentant heart. Praise God that He is able to love us when others reject us. Reaffirm Christ's love to each child as you value and accept each one in your class.

Teacher Tips:

You may want to bring in a large bowl to show each experiment to the children, and then let them replicate the experiment themselves. It works best for children to have their own cups for the experiments.

An area near a sink or outdoor water faucet works best. If you're indoors, prepare for potential water spills by removing items that could be damaged, or covering the area with newspaper or plastic.

Use the opportunity of choosing helpers to reinforce good behavior. Choose a helper and compliment the child on what they did or said that followed the classroom rules or showed a helpful attitude.

After seeing the pepper move away from the liquid soap, continue to watch what happens after a minute or so. The soap spreads out and the pepper starts to move back towards the center. You can liken this to a situation where people get to know someone and find out the person they thought they didn't like was really very nice.

Variations to the Experiment:

Each time the children try a variation, they'll need a clean cup. If reusing the same cup, offer paper towels to wipe the cup clean. You don't want to have any soap remaining in the cup that might ruin the next experiment.

Try different substances to see if they'll repel the pepper or make it come together. See if other spices work like the pepper.

Materials List:

Experiment #1:

- ❍ Large bowl or individual cups for the children
- ❍ Water
- ❍ Toothpick
- ❍ Black pepper
- ❍ Eyedropper
- ❍ Liquid dish detergent

Experiment #2:

- ❍ Large bowl or individual cups for the children
- ❍ Water
- ❍ Toothpick
- ❍ Eyedropper
- ❍ Cooking oil
- ❍ Food coloring
- ❍ Optional: paper towels

Note: Use the same bowl and eyedropper for both experiments, but clean them before reusing them.

INVESTIGATION

Experiment #1

1. Fill the bowl three-quarters full with water. Sprinkle pepper onto the surface.
2. Let children use a toothpick to try to get the pepper to move to the sides of the bowl. The pepper should keep floating on the surface. Point out how the pepper is like the Jewish people who went to listen to Jesus.
3. Use the eyedropper to drop the dish detergent into the center of the pepper. One drop is enough to send the pepper instantly away to the edges. Discuss how the drop of detergent was like Zacchaeus, and how the Jews treated him.
4. Give each child a cup and let the children try the experiment for themselves.

Experiment #2

1. Fill the bowl three-quarters full with water. Add a few drops of food coloring.
2. Use the eyedropper to put several drops of the cooking oil onto the water. Discuss how Jesus accepts everyone and brings them together in Him.
3. Watch as the drops of oil come together to form one big drop. If you need to speed up the experiment, use the toothpick to swirl the water a little so the oil drops come together. Also, after the oil forms one large drop, you can shake the water and break up the oil to start the experiment again.
4. Give each child a cup and let the children try the experiment for themselves.

WHY DOES IT WORK?

Experiment #1

The water has a strong surface tension almost like an invisible skin. The surface tension or invisible skin holds the pepper on top of the water. The liquid soap breaks the surface tension so water pulls the pepper away from the soap. If you watch carefully, the liquid soap will slowly spread out and form a thin layer on the water that eventually starts to bring the pepper back from the edges.

Experiment #2

The oil floats on top of the water. The water molecules are called polar molecules because there is more positive charge in one part of the molecule and more negative charge in another part of the molecule. The oil molecules are more evenly distributed, so they're called non-polar molecules. The polar molecules of water stick together and keep the non-polar oil molecules away. The oil gathers together into one big blob.

END WITH A BANG

- **Which experiment did you like best? Why?**
- **Why did the pepper move away from the soap?** *(The soap broke the water tension and caused the pepper to move away from it.)*
- **Why did the oil drops move together?** *(The oil moved together because the water wouldn't let it get between the water molecules.)*

These experiments remind us of the Bible story. The Jews didn't like Zacchaeus; they wanted to stay away from him just like the pepper stayed away from the drop of soap. But Jesus accepted Zacchaeus. Jesus accepts everyone and wants each of us to be part of His family. That's similar to how the one drop of oil joined with another and soon all the oil drops had come together in a large drop.

- **How do you feel when someone accepts you and welcomes you?**
- **How do we know Jesus accepts everyone who comes to Him?** *(He came to save all people who are lost, He showed acceptance, He loves everyone, etc.)*
- **What can you do to help accept people like Jesus did?**

VANISHING FACE

Your brain plays a trick on you in this experiment.

Bible Basis: Luke 24:1-12; John 10:17-18

MEMORY VERSE:
Because I live, you also will live.
John 14:19

BIBLE BACKGROUND

The fact that Jesus' tomb was sealed wasn't unusual. Gravesites were routinely sealed to prevent vandalism and to keep animals from disturbing the entombed body. The Romans authorized the sealing of Jesus' tomb, which prevented the possibility that zealous followers might steal the body. The stone that sealed the tomb would have probably rested in a downward slanting track or ramp making it easy to close off the tomb. It would have required many men to push the large boulder uphill to gain access to the tomb. This fact also dispels any belief that Jesus might not have been dead and removed the stone Himself.

The speed of Jesus' burial was due to the impending sundown on Friday that marked the start of the Jewish Sabbath. Even though the Jewish leaders didn't accept Jesus as God's Son, they respected God's command to obey the Sabbath. When the Sabbath ended on Saturday at sundown, it would have been too dark to prepare the body with the traditional burial customs.

Women—not the disciples who remained hidden and fearful of arrest—discovered the empty tomb. It's interesting to note that these same disciples witnessed Jesus raise Lazarus from the dead, yet doubted Jesus' ability to fulfill what He promised for Himself. Don't let any doubts linger in your mind—Christ the Lord is risen! Let His resurrection release your faith to believe Him for great and powerful things.

Teacher Tips:

Have children determine which of their eyes is dominant and use the mirror with that eye. To find eye dominance: Hold your hands palm-side down, one on top of the other, with thumbs and fingers overlapping to form a one-inch triangle. Hold your hands about a foot from your face and pick a spot on the wall, or a picture, that you see in the center of the triangle. Without moving your hands, close one eye. If the object moves from the center of the triangle, you've found your weak eye.

If closing one eye at a time proves difficult, there's a simple fix. Form the same triangle mentioned above with your hands. Without moving your head, slowly move the triangle closer to your face. Keep the object you're focusing on in the center of the triangle as you bring your hands toward you. When your hands reach your face, the triangle will be in front of your dominant eye.

This experiment works best if you stare intently. Hold the mirror at a 45-degree angle between your nose and eye (roughly halfway between them). Help kids angle the mirror to get the best results.

Remind kids to not walk around the room with the mirror over one eye because they could easily walk into someone or something.

Variations to the Experiment:

Have several small pocket-size mirrors so pairs of children can try the experiment without the plain background. If the children stand face to face, the child with the mirror should wiggle the mirror and then should see the other child's face on the wall or picture.

Materials List:

- ❍ Handheld mirror
- ❍ 2 sheets of plain white poster board or 2 white bed sheets
- ❍ 2 chairs

INVESTIGATION

1. Find a location with two blank walls at right angles to each other, or use the poster board or sheets to create two blank spaces. Ask volunteers to hold the sheets or poster board.
2. Set the two chairs close together and facing each other. One chair should be against one of the walls. Choose two volunteers to sit in the chairs. Note: You may need to move the chairs depending on the dominant eye of each child. The blank space should be on the side of the child's dominant eye.
3. Give the mirror to one of the seated children. Let the child hold the mirror at a 45-degree angle between his eye and nose. The blank wall should be seen in the mirror when the opposite eye is closed.
4. With both eyes open and staring at the other child, the child should move the hand on the side with the mirror so the hand makes movements like erasing a chalkboard. The face of the other child should look like it's being erased.
5. Switch and let the other partner try the experiment. Allow time for each child to try the experiment. If you have a large class, bring several mirrors and have more than one pair participate at a time.

WHY DOES IT WORK?

Since our eyes are separated by our nose, they see things at different angles. The brain takes the two images and combines them into one picture. When the mirror diverts one of the eyes to a blank wall, the other eye's picture registers on the brain. The movement of the hand or the mirror triggers the brain to focus on the movement. Then the brain combines the places where the movement was with the image of the face. This gives the effect that part of the face has vanished. Then the face completely reappears when the movement stops.

END WITH A BANG

- Did the effect work when you tried the experiment? Why or why not?
- Why was the mirror necessary? *(The mirror tricked the eye and made it difficult to combine the two different images.)*
- Why do you think the face looked like it vanished? *(The movement of the hand or mirror tricked the brain to transfer the movement to the face.)*

The mirror helped your eyes play a trick on your brain. When Jesus' body was missing from the guarded tomb, it seemed like someone was playing a trick. However, Jesus' resurrection was no trick—it was real!

- When has someone played a trick on you that seemed real?
- How would you have reacted if you had seen Jesus' empty tomb?

COLOR-CHANGING FRUIT-AID

Explore how colored water mysteriously goes clear.

Bible Basis: John 3:1-21

MEMORY VERSE:
God so loved the world that he gave his one and only Son, that whoever believes in him shall not perish but have eternal life.
John 3:16

BIBLE BACKGROUND

Jesus wasn't popular among the Pharisees of His day. They resented Jesus' popularity among the Jews. These religious Jewish men were more conservative in how the law was interpreted than the Sadducees. A ruling council called the Sanhedrin consisted of 70 teachers of the law, both Pharisees and Sadducees.

One of the Pharisees who also belonged to the Sanhedrin chose to secretly meet with Jesus. In this nighttime meeting, Nicodemus admitted to knowing about Jesus miraculously changing water to wine (John 2:1–11) and clearing the temple of money changers (John 2:13–17). He also acknowledged what few religious men dared to speak—Jesus must be a teacher sent from God. Later, when the Jews wanted Jesus arrested, Nicodemus questioned the right of the Pharisees to condemn a man without an opportunity to listen to him (John 7:50–52).

Jesus first used the term "born again" while talking to Nicodemus. Nicodemus misunderstood and questioned how he could experience physical birth again. Maybe the children in your class have similar misconceptions about being born again or becoming a Christian. Use this opportunity to show them the life-changing effect Jesus has when they accept His gift of salvation and become born again.

Teacher Tips:

Immediately after the experiment, dispose of the solution so no child tries to drink it. If you don't have access to a sink, have a container full of dirt and pour the bleach water into the container.

This experiment must be performed either outside or in a well-ventilated area.

It's vital that only adults handle the bleach and the bleach solution.

Remember that bleach will discolor clothes or carpet. Use a plastic tablecloth and have old towels ready to clean up any spills. Monitor the bleach container at all times. Avoid the bleach coming in contact with skin or eyes.

Variations to the Experiment:

Test more substances to see if they'll return the colored water to clear water.

Also, try adding bleach to the milk and lemon juice.

Materials List:

- ❍ Clear pitcher of water
- ❍ Red-colored powdered drink mix
- ❍ 5 clear drinking glasses
- ❍ Eyedropper
- ❍ Liquid bleach (bring a small amount in a well-sealed jar)
- ❍ 1 c. additional water
- ❍ 1 c. lemon juice
- ❍ 1 c. milk
- ❍ 1 c. sugar
- ❍ Optional: extra cups, large spoon

INVESTIGATION

1. Show the children the pitcher of water and talk about how pure water is like a life without sin.
2. Add the red-colored drink mix and talk about how sin comes into our lives. Let the children name sins that might come into a child's life.
3. Pour the drink into several clear glasses. Talk about how a person's life has sin, and the person might try several ways to remove the sin.
4. Ask a child to try to change the water back to clear again by adding more water to one of the glasses. Choose another volunteer to try adding lemon juice to the second glass. Let another child try adding sugar to the third glass, and someone can add milk to the fourth glass.
5. Explain the only way to remove sin is asking Jesus for forgiveness and believing on Him. Add a few drops of bleach into the water mixture in the glass. The liquid should turn clear.
6. Pour that mixture back into the container and watch the drink turn clear. One by one, ask children to pour the other test samples back into the pitcher. After all of the children have seen the mixture, dispose of the bleach water.

WHY DOES IT WORK?

The bleach was able to remove the color in the water because it contains sodium hypochlorite. As the chemicals in the dye interact with the oxygen released from the bleach, a clear solution is created.

END WITH A BANG

- **Why did the bleach remove the color from the water?** *(The chemicals in dye react with the oxygen released from the bleach and turn the water clear again.)*
- **What else does bleach do?** *(Bleach takes the color from clothes, carpets, and other things it comes in contact with. It can also burn skin or eyes.)*
- **Can other compounds remove color from something?**

How wonderful that God can take away the sin in our lives, even more effectively than bleach removed the color from the water. Nicodemus wanted eternal life and he went to the right person—Jesus! We can take our sins to Jesus and He removes them so that we can have eternal life.

- **Why does Jesus want to take away our sins?** *(He wants us to live in heaven with Him, and we can't unless our sin is forgiven through Him. Only He can forgive our sins, and He will because He loves us.)*
- **What does Jesus offer?** *(Jesus offers eternal life.)*

OVERFLOWING HELPER

Yeast powers this explosive experiment.

Bible Basis: John 13:1-3; 14:16-19, 25-26; 15:26; 16:7

MEMORY VERSE:
I will ask the Father, and he will give you another Counselor to be with you forever—the Spirit of truth.
John 14:16–17

BIBLE BACKGROUND

Jesus promised the Holy Spirit would come to believers (John 7:39). While Jesus remained on earth, the disciples could receive help and teaching directly from Him. Jesus' ascension into heaven created the need for a Divine Helper to remain on earth. Details about the Spirit were given during the Last Supper (John 14:16–17, 26). In this passage, Jesus called the Holy Spirit the Counselor, a legal term meaning counsel for the defense.

Previously, the disciples had shown their lack of faith in Christ and His promise to come back to life after His death. Jesus' followers displayed great faith in the promise of the Holy Spirit when they waited in Jerusalem as Jesus had instructed (Acts 1:4). The timing of the Holy Spirit's arrival was during the Feast of Pentecost (Acts 2:1–4). During this feast, gifts of the harvest were given to God. How appropriate that God used this day to give Christians the gift of the Holy Spirit!

Jesus returned to heaven, but you're not alone—the Holy Sprit is with you. As the Spirit leads you, you'll help the children see an example of the power of God at work in your life.

Teacher Tips:

This safe and fun experiment is sometimes referred to as "elephant toothpaste." Several videos on the Internet show elephant toothpaste erupting and spraying all over. Those videos use hydrogen peroxide with a much higher percentage of chemicals (30%) not found over the counter. The hydrogen peroxide available over the counter has a 3% chemical content and isn't dangerous.

Start the yeast first so it has five to ten minutes to proof, or get foamy. If you want to try several variations, get several yeast cups started at the same time.

This experiment can be done in a sink or a large bowl. If you're doing this experiment outside, place an open trash bag on the ground and set the experiment in the trash bag. When the experiment foams over, it will stay within the trash bag for easy cleanup.

Variations to the Experiment:

Try different containers and different amounts of hydrogen peroxide and yeast.

Use a stopwatch to time how long the mixture keeps foaming. See if there are differences in the length of the foaming when altering the experiment.

Materials List:

- ❍ Empty bottle (16-oz. or 1-liter works well)
- ❍ 1 c. hydrogen peroxide
- ❍ ¼ c. liquid soap
- ❍ Funnel
- ❍ Bowl
- ❍ ¼ c. warm water
- ❍ 2 ½ tsp. yeast
- ❍ 1 tsp. sugar
- ❍ Food coloring

INVESTIGATION

1. Mix the yeast, sugar, and water together in a bowl at the beginning of class so the yeast has five to ten minutes to proof, or get foamy.
2. Add a few drops of food coloring into the bottle. Use the funnel to pour the foamy yeast mixture into the bottle. If it doesn't go down the funnel easily, pour the liquid soap mixture into the funnel to help the yeast mixture slide easily into the bottle.
3. Pour in the hydrogen peroxide and watch the colored foam build up and flow over the sides.

WHY DOES IT WORK?

Hydrogen peroxide contains two parts hydrogen and two parts oxygen. It continuously breaks down into water and oxygen. The yeast is the catalyst, speeding up the reaction and causing the hydrogen peroxide to decompose faster and bubble. The soap creates an extra foamy texture that lasts longer.

Note: When hydrogen peroxide is added to a cut, it bubbles because body fluids catalyze the decomposition.

END WITH A BANG

- **Why did the foam rise?** *(The pressure kept building and pushed it upward.)*
- **What did the yeast do?** *(The yeast made the hydrogen peroxide react quickly.)*
- **Why did it turn foamy?** *(The liquid foams because the hydrogen peroxide keeps breaking down into water and oxygen.)*
- **What would you try differently next time?**

The hydrogen peroxide needed help to create the fun foam. It couldn't do it alone. The yeast made the hydrogen quickly start working to make the foam. Sometimes, it's hard to do what God asks without a little extra power from God. We have that power available to help us—the Holy Spirit!

- **When have you asked God for help?**
- **Who did God send to be our Helper?** *(The Holy Spirit.)*

HOVERCRAFT

Watch your problems move away and become something good!

Bible Basis: 2 Corinthians 12:7-10; Matthew 6:10-11

MEMORY VERSE:
Your kingdom come, your will be done on earth as it is in heaven.
Matthew 6:10

BIBLE BACKGROUND

Bible scholars don't know the source of Paul's "thorn in [his] flesh." Some speculate it could have been a physical ailment such as an eye problem, epilepsy, malaria, or headaches. Another theory asserts it could have been a spiritual problem or addictive sin that Paul could not conquer. Paul himself called it a "messenger of Satan" (2 Cor. 12:7).

Of course Paul would have liked his prayer answered by a healing, but God's answer is always best. God certainly could have healed Paul from his problem, yet look at the strength it built in him. Paul turned to God for power and found that his weakness provided the opportunity to see just how powerful God was. Rather than use his problem to hide from ministry or people, Paul boasted in his weakness.

You may not be ready to boast about your problems or weaknesses, but just think of your powerful witness in telling others how God has strengthened and helped you.

Teacher Tips:

Prior to class, glue the water bottle lid to the CD so that the pop-open side is up. Allow a bit of time before class for the glue to harden.

Choose a clean, smooth surface such as a countertop or tabletop. Be aware that dirt on a smooth floor will cause friction for the hovercraft.

Have contests; use a stopwatch to see the longest time a hovercraft moves and a yardstick to determine the farthest.

Always have extra balloons in case of breakage.

Variations to the Experiment:

Try a variety of different materials for the hovercraft, such as thick paper, cardboard, a foam plate, a paper plate, clear acetate, etc. Cut a three by three-inch square and attach the water bottle lid to the square you're testing. Make a chart on the board and let children fill in the results after testing each material.

A hovercraft usually goes across water. Set out a large tub of water and let kids launch their hovercrafts on the water. Have children compare and contrast the water to the floor or other surface used.

Play air hockey with the hovercrafts. Create a small hockey-playing area with goals. You may want to mark the boundaries with masking tape.

Materials List:

- ❍ Old CD-ROM or CD (1 for each child)
- ❍ Balloon, 12" (1 for each child)
- ❍ Screw-on water bottle cap which pops up to open and down to close (1 for each child)
- ❍ Hot-glue gun, super glue, or wide tape
- ❍ Permanent markers (1 for each child)

INVESTIGATION

1. Make sure the water bottle lid is in the closed position. Blow up the balloon and place it over the water bottle lid.
2. Set the hovercraft on a smooth surface. Lift up on the water bottle lid (through the balloon) to release the air. Watch the hovercraft begin to move. Ask the children if they've played air hockey and seen the puck move because of the air coming up from the table.
3. Give each child a CD with the lid attached. Tell the children that the CDs represent a problem in our lives that we want God to help with or to take away, just like Paul's thorn in his flesh. Have children wear paint shirts, then use a marker to write on the CD their personal concern or problem.
4. Give each child a balloon and discuss how God can lift our problems and change them into something good. Write "God" on each balloon and give each child a balloon.
5. Let the kids blow up the balloons, attach them to the lids, and then use their hovercrafts.

WHY DOES IT WORK?

The hovercraft lifts because escaping air from the balloon pushes out from under the CD. As the CD lifts it's able to move because it encounters very little friction. When the air runs out of the balloon, the hovercraft stops moving.

END WITH A BANG

- **What does it mean to hover?** *(To hover means to glide or be suspended in the air.)*
- **Why did the hovercraft move?** *(The air from the balloon went out under the CD and pushed it up.)*
- **Why does it slow down or stop?** *(It slows when there is more friction caused by less air pressure from the balloon.)*
- **What could you use to design a hovercraft that didn't use a balloon for power?** *(Use a motor or a fan.)*

The CD is like our problems. We can ask God to take away our problems. But sometimes He turns our problems into something we can live with, or maybe even see something good about them. So when we turn our problems over to God, His answers are the best answer.

- **When have you seen God turn someone's problem into a good thing?**
- **What problem would you like God to turn into something good?**

Let's pray and ask God to surprise us by turning our problems into something we can praise Him for!

PRAYER CHAIR

Build a chair with paper cups.

Bible Basis: 1 Timothy 2:1-8

MEMORY VERSE:
Always keep on praying for all the saints.
Ephesians 6:18

BIBLE BACKGROUND

Paul wrote 1 and 2 Timothy and Titus as advice letters for the pastoral care of the churches. Timothy had been left in charge of the church in Ephesus to help administrate and deal with its problems. Paul most likely had written this letter after his arrival in Macedonia. The relationship between the two men was like father and son.

Paul stated the need to pray for those in authority. At the time of his writing, the Roman emperor Nero was ruler; he was the first Roman emperor to persecute the Christian church. It may seem like a call to pray for the emperor's removal, but Paul clearly asked for prayers that Christians would lead peaceful lives that displayed godliness and holiness (1 Tim. 2:2). How wonderful if we would pray for our leaders, and then live godly lives that allow unbelievers to see God at work in our lives and desire a relationship with Him!

We have a privilege to pray for others, and hopefully your classroom is a place of prayer. As you model prayers for the class, also allow opportunities for the children to voice their prayer requests.

Teacher Tips:

Paper cups work best. Even the tiny three-ounce cups work well. Figure about 12–20 cups per child. It's better to have too many than for the children to be disappointed or not have an opportunity to try the experiment.

If you don't have cardboard squares, check with a grocery store for boxes that can be cut up into 12" squares.

Sitting on the cups is safer than standing. Make sure you do an activity like this in an open area where no child could fall and hit a desk or cupboard.

Variations to the Experiment:

Test it out. Before testing the cups, let the students vote on which cup types they think will be the strongest and the weakest.

Have the children work in small groups of three to four. Give each group a different size or kind of cup (tiny, paper, foam, plastic, 16-oz. size, etc.). Let the children see how few cups they can sit on without the cups crushing. Afterward, let each group share what they discovered.

It's possible, and fun, to build a double-decker chair out of two levels of cups and cardboard. For safety, don't allow the children to build higher than two levels.

Materials List:

For each "prayer chair":

- 12–20 disposable drinking cups (paper, plastic, foam, 3 oz., 16 oz., etc.)
- Cardboard square (12" x 12")

INVESTIGATION

1. Place a cup on the floor with the cup opening against the floor. Balance the cardboard on top of the cup. Ask the group what they think will happen if someone tries to sit on the cup. Choose a volunteer to sit on the cardboard and cup.
2. Now place on the floor 12–20 cups (depending on the size of the cups). Lay the cardboard over the cups and ask the children to predict the results. Choose a volunteer to sit on the cups.
3. Remove two to four of the cups. Place the cardboard on top of the cups and let a child sit on the cups.
4. Continue removing cups until they crush. Once a cup is crushed, don't reuse it.
5. Try the experiment again with a different type of cup.
6. Allow time for each child to try sitting on the chair. Have the children pray for that person, silently or out loud, as he or she sits. Challenge the students. By the time the chair collapses, see if they can pray for as many people as the number of cups needed to make the chair work. (They may need to think of others outside your group.)

WHY DOES IT WORK?

If you stand or sit on one cup, it will smash because of the weight that is compressing the cup. As you spread out the cups and cover them with a piece of cardboard, your weight is distributed. Each cup has to hold less of your weight.

END WITH A BANG

- **Did you think the cups could hold you up?**
- **What was the fewest number of cups that held you up?**
- **Why did the cups hold you up?** *(The cups held a person up because the weight was spread out. Each cup had to hold up a smaller amount when there were more cups.)*

Sitting on the cups was easiest when you had a lot of cups under the cardboard. Each cup could represent someone who needs your prayers. When you pray for someone, you're giving that person a gift. You're taking him or her before God who cares about their needs. The more prayers you pray for a variety of people—the better!

- **Who are some people we might not usually think of for whom we can pray?**
- **Have you experienced answers to your prayers? Tell us about them.**

TIGHTROPE WALKERS

You'll respect these balancing leaders!

Bible Basis: 1 Timothy 1:1-5; 3:15; 4:6, 12; 2 Timothy 1:1-7; 2:1-3; 3:14-15; Acts 16:1-3; 17:13-15

MEMORY VERSE:
Respect those who work hard among you.
1 Thessalonians 5:12

BIBLE BACKGROUND

Timothy's parents were a Greek man and a Jewish woman who lived in Lystra, in modern-day Turkey. Jewish law stated that a child born to a Jewish mother was a Jew, so Timothy would have been raised according to Jewish customs. He would have learned the Scriptures beginning at the age of five.

We know that Timothy's mother and grandmother were Christians. Their conversion might have been a result of Paul and Barnabas's first missionary trip. (The Bible doesn't mention the faith of Timothy's father.)

Paul refers to Timothy as "my true son in the faith" (1 Tim. 1:2). He also views Timothy as "young" (1 Tim. 4:12), even though Timothy might have been in his thirties. Timothy was challenged by Paul to set an example in his speech, life, love, faith, and purity (1 Tim. 4:12). No wonder he was a respected leader! Wouldn't it be wonderful if today's leaders aspired to fulfill that same list?

You can be a positive example to the children as you speak respectfully to them and of those in leadership. Remember, showing respect to someone doesn't mean you agree with everything they say or do—it shows you are obeying God (Rom. 13:7)!

Teacher Tips:

If you have an opportunity to make some "leaders" ahead of time, try to get photos of various leaders in your church. Cut out the face and glue it onto the cardboard figure.

If you have a large class, you may want to write the names on the figures before class time.

Corrugated cardboard is the material of brown packing boxes. Stores may give you boxes already broken down; these will work just fine because you'll cut the boxes apart even further.

Variations to the Experiment:

Try cutting some leader shapes with different-shaped bases rather than straight, such as rounded bottom, zigzagged, slanted, or wavy.

Thread actually works well and the tightrope-walker figures can slide back and forth easily on it. Encourage the children to test other materials and report which one works best. Kids could try yarn, string, twine, or clear nylon thread.

Materials List:

- ❍ Corrugated cardboard
- ❍ Chenille stems (1 for each child)
- ❍ Metal washers of various sizes
- ❍ Paper clips in 2 sizes
- ❍ Thread
- ❍ Scissors
- ❍ Markers or pencils

INVESTIGATION

1. Before class, cut out several pieces of cardboard in the simple shape of a person. Make a circle for the head and shoulders that slant down to the chest area, making a straight cut along the bottom. Use corrugated cardboard with the lines or grooves going horizontally, not vertically. Cut out as many figures as there are children. Vary the height from two to six inches tall, with a width of about four inches.
2. Ask the children to name some of your church's leaders. Write a leader's name on each cutout and give it to a child to quickly draw in a face.
3. Give each child a chenille stem to slide through one of the corrugated waves (the honeycomb-like openings in-between the outer layers) in the cardboard.
4. Discuss tightrope walkers children have seen and how they balanced. Explain that students will be experimenting to find out how to balance the cardboard figures and get them to move back and forth on the tightrope.
5. Divide the class into groups of four (try to make sure each group has a variety of sizes of the figures). Give each group a spool of thread about five feet long. Also set out a variety of washers and paper clips.
6. Have two children hold the thread taut by pinching it between their fingers. Remind kids not to break the thread, but the thread shouldn't be limp either.
7. The other two children should test their figures to see if they balance. Encourage kids to try adding washers or paper clips to achieve balance. Also let students experiment with moving the chenille stem higher up the figure, or try cutting the chenille stem shorter.
8. When children achieve a well-balanced figure, have the thread holders slant the thread a couple of inches (one child raises and the other child lowers) and watch the figure walk back and forth, balancing on the thread.
9. After four to five minutes, kids should switch places so the children who held the thread are now doing the experiment.

WHY DOES IT WORK?

The tightrope is an axis and the performer tries to keep his center of mass directly above the wire, so as not to rotate around the axis. A real-life tightrope walker carries a balancing pole that could be as long as 39 feet and weigh as much as 31 pounds. The pole helps lower the center of gravity, sometimes even lower than the wire. It also delays the person's moment of inertia (giving time for the performer to correct any wobbles and restore balance).

END WITH A BANG

- **What size figure worked the best?** *(Smaller should work better.)*
- **What position worked best for the arms?** *(Longer and below the thread works best.)*
- **Did the paper clips or washers make it easier to balance or harder?** *(Weight helps achieve balance.)*

It was hard work to get the tightrope-walker figures to balance. It's also hard work for our church leaders to balance their many jobs and responsibilities, but they do a great job.

- **What qualities do you respect about our church leaders?** *(they love God, speak truthfully, help others, etc.)*
- **How can we show respect to our church leaders?** *(listen to them, speak nicely, don't argue with them, help them, etc.)*

RED/GREEN VEGGIE REACTOR

Red cabbage sorts out the acids from the bases.

Bible Basis: Philemon 1-25

MEMORY VERSE:
Listen to advice and accept instruction, and in the end you will be wise.
Proverbs 19:20

BIBLE BACKGROUND

While Christians today would abhor slavery, in Paul's day slavery was commonplace. According to Roman law, slaves weren't considered legal persons and therefore were not allowed to represent themselves in court, own or inherit property, or select a mate. A slave was subject to the master's treatment—or mistreatment. Freedom could be purchased or given by the master.

Onesimus was a slave who had run away from his owner, Philemon, a Greek landowner living in the city of Colosse. Running away was a crime legally punishable by death. Jews were allowed to own slaves, but the Old Testament urged kindness toward slaves (Deut. 15:12–18; Lev. 25:53).

Paul brought Onesimus to faith in Christ while they were in prison, and Paul saw this onetime slave as a brother, not a possession. Onesimus also became a brother in Christ with Philemon, and their relationship became one based on forgiveness and acceptance instead of ownership and slavery.

The name Onesimus means helpful or useful. We read Paul's play on words in verse 11 of Philemon, "He was useless…but has become useful." The spiritual guidance received by the slave allowed him to be dear to Paul's heart (Philem. 1:12).

You have a wonderful opportunity to help and guide children to make wise, godly decisions. Don't be afraid to ask other Christians for advice or counsel, but remember—God gives wisdom to those who ask Him (Col. 1:9)!

Teacher Tips:

You may want to blend the cabbage and water at home and bring the mixture to class. Red cabbage has a very strong odor, so you might want to warn the class. Keep the mixture refrigerated until you take it to class.

Remind children that these solutions are not drinks, but chemical experiments.

Cover the table area with newspaper or plastic tablecloth. Red cabbage juice may stain clothing, but easily washes off skin with warm water and soap.

Variations to the Experiment:

Mix more than one substance with the cabbage indicator. When you discover how lemon juice responds, add baking soda to see if the reaction changes.

Have children make a chart and record the results.

Note: Don't combine household-cleaning products together.

Materials List:

- ❍ Blender
- ❍ Strainer
- ❍ Red cabbage
- ❍ Clear drinking glasses or other small glasses (1 per chemical test)
- ❍ Vinegar
- ❍ Powdered laundry detergent
- ❍ Paper
- ❍ Pen
- ❍ Spoons or coffee stirrers
- ❍ Chemicals to test such as: lemon juice, milk, salt, sugar, baking soda, stomach antacids, orange juice, soap, ketchup, coffee, etc.

INVESTIGATION

1. Remove six big cabbage leaves or chop about two cups worth of cabbage and place in a blender half full of boiling water. Note: Be careful of liquid spurting from the blender. Blend until all is liquefied. Pour the mixture through a strainer to remove any solids. Your red cabbage liquid is ready to be used. Note: This step may be done ahead of time at home.

2. Pour cabbage liquid into two clear glasses. Add vinegar to one jar and stir. The mixture should turn red. Put a paper under this glass and label the paper "Acid." Add laundry detergent to the other glass and it should turn green. Put a paper under this glass and label it "Base." These are your samples to help compare each test result.

3. Now you're ready to experiment with finding out which substances are bases or acids. Set out other glasses and add cabbage juice.

4. Add a substance to a glass and stir. Compare the color of the mixture to the two samples to determine if the substance is an acid or a base. Note: If there is no color change or it turns blue, the result is neutral. Pink color indicates a weak acid and yellow indicates a strong base.

WHY DOES IT WORK?

The cabbage is an indicator because it shows what chemicals other substances are made of. When red cabbage juice is mixed with a base or an alkaline, it turns the mixture green. When cabbage juice is mixed with an acid, the mixture turns red. If there is a neutral substance like water, there will be no color change.

Note: Your body has an acid or alkaline level measurable through urine. Interestingly, substances that are highly acidic like orange juice metabolize in the body and cause the urine to become alkaline.

END WITH A BANG

- **Which chemical reactions surprised you?**
- **Why did the substance change color to red?** *(Red shows the substance has acid in it.)*
- **Why did the substance change color to green?** *(Green shows the substance is a base or an alkaline.)*

It's good to know when something contains an acid that could be harmful. The cabbage helped us know which substances had acid in them. We can turn to other Christians when we need help in knowing if something is right or wrong. When we listen to good Christian advice, we can make wise choices.

- **Who do you usually ask for advice?**
- **Why do you think we should ask Christians for help making wise choices?** *(They can help us understand how to follow God's Word.)*

Fun and Freaky Science
SCRIPTURE AND TOPIC INDEX

The following index allows you to use this book with any curriculum.
Simply find the Scripture your lesson is based on or the Topic you are teaching

Fun and Freaky Science
CORRELATION CHART

Each activity correlates to a Unit and Lesson in the curriculum lines shown below.

For further help on how to use the chart see page 5.

Title	Page	Scripture Reference	**David C. Cook BIL** **LifeLINKS to God** **New Life** **College Press** **Reformation Press** **Wesley** **Anglican**	**Echoes** **The Cross**
Volcano Creations	6	Genesis 1:1-31; Psalm 111:2, 7	Unit 1, Lesson 1	Unit 1, Lesson 1
Whirlybird Fliers	10	Genesis 1:20-25	Unit 1, Lesson 3	Unit 1, Lesson 3
Vanishing Act	14	Genesis 2:15-17; 3:1-24	Unit 2, Lesson 5	Unit 2, Lesson 5
Water Wheelies	18	Genesis 6:9—7:24	Unit 2, Lesson 7	Unit 2, Lesson 7
Lead On	22	Genesis 11:31—12:9; 17:1-8, 15; Hebrews 11:8	Unit 3, Lesson 9	Unit 2, Lesson 10
Wierd and Wonderful Goo	26	Genesis 18: 1-16; 21:1-6	Unit 3, Lesson 11	Unit 3, Lesson 11
Candy Blast Off	30	Genesis 24	Unit 3, Lesson 13	Unit 3, Lesson 12
Get the Picture?	50	Matthew 1:18-25; Luke 1:26-38; John 1:1	Unit 4, Lesson 2	
Rejoicin' Raisins & Glad Grapes	62	Luke 2:21-38	Unit 4, Lesson 4	Unit 4, Lesson 4
Ice Cube Towers	66	Luke 2:41-52	Unit 5, Lesson 6	Unit 5, Lesson 6
Which Way Out?	70	Luke 4:1-13; Hebrews 2:18; 4:15	Unit 5, Lesson 8	
Breathless Balloon Blow Up	74	Luke 7:1-10	Unit 6, Lesson 10	
Wave Watcher	54	Mark 4:1-2a, 35-41	Unit 6, Lesson 12	Unit 6, Lesson 11
Color Changing Kool-Aid	86	John 3:1-21	Unit 7, Lesson 1	Unit 8, Lesson 8
Water Wonders	78	Luke 19:1-10	Unit 7, Lesson 3	Unit 7, Lesson 1
Vanishing Face	82	Luke 24:1-12; John 10:17-18	Unit 8, Lesson 5	
Overflowing Helper	90	John 13:1-3; 14:16-19, 25-26; 15:26; 16:7	Unit 8, Lesson 7	
Crazy Camera	34	Genesis 25:27-34; 27:1-45	Unit 9, Lesson 9	Unit 9, Lesson 9
Gel Be Gone	38	Genesis 37	Unit 9, Lesson 11	Unit 9, Lesson 11
Overcoming Power	42	Genesis 41:14—47:12	Unit 9, Lesson 13	Unit 9, Lesson 13
Tightrope Walkers	102	2 Timothy 1:1-7; 2:1-3; 3:14-15; Acts 16:1-3; 17:13-15; 1 Timothy 1:1-5; 3:15; 4:6, 12	Unit 10, Lesson 2	
Green/Red Veggie Reader	90	Philemon 1-25	Unit 10, Lesson 4	Unit 10, Lesson 1
Hovercraft	94	2 Corinthians 12:7-10; Matthew 6:10- 11	Unit 11, Lesson 6	
Prayer Chair	98	1 Timothy 2:1-8	Unit 11, Lesson 8	
Hidden Message	46	Deuteronomy 5:1-7; 6:5-9; 28:1-14; 31:9—32:47; Hebrews 1:1	Unit 12, Lesson 10	Unit 12, Lesson 10
Colossal Candy Construction	58	Luke 1:1-4; John 4:42; 20:28-31, Matthew 26:63-64; Mark 8:27-30	Unit 12, Lesson 12	